JASPER PARK LODGE

by Cyndi Smith

Canadian Cataloguing in Publication Data

Smith, Cyndi, 1956–
    Jasper Park Lodge: in the heart of the Canadian Rockies

First ed. published Jasper, Alta.: C. Smith, 1985. Includes
bibliographical references and index.
ISBN 0-9692457-9-3

    1. Jasper Park Lodge -- History.   I. Title.

FC3664.J3S65 1995   647.947123'32   C95-900285-5
F1079.J3S65 1995

© 1985 by Cyndi Smith   All rights reserved.

ISBN 0-9692457-9-3

First printing 1985.
Second printing 1995.
Printed and bound in Canada.

Published by: Coyote Books
              P.O. Box 3397
              Canmore, Alberta
              T0L 0M0
              Canada

JASPER PARK LODGE

In the heart of the Canadian Rockies

by Cyndi Smith

Coyote Books, Canmore, Alberta

For my mother,
who fostered in me
a keen appreciation of
books and history.

Instead of an incongruous, many-storied structure of steel and stone, with towers and turrets and terraces which would be wholly out of place in such a setting, the architects had the good taste to build a long, low-roofed, rambling hostelry of logs and boulders — the largest log building in the world, it is claimed — so that there is nothing in its appearance to form a discordant note.

- Alexander E. Powell
Marches of the North (1931)

Author's Note

Throughout this book I make reference to Jasper Park Lodge in three different ways — using its full name, the first letters only (JPL) and simply "the Lodge." These are completely interchangeable. "The Lodge" refers to the complete resort, while "the lodge," not capitalized, refers only to the main central building.

Two other abbreviations were also used where appropriate: Grand Trunk Pacific Railway (GTPR) and Canadian National Railways (CNR).

References for quoted material, and any notes, appear at the back of the book, by chapter.

Addendum — 1995

In the decade since this book was first published there have been a number of changes at the resort. The biggest change is that Canadian Pacific Hotels & Resorts purchased the Lodge from Canadian National Railways in 1988. The new management brought with them many ideas, one of which was to turn JPL into a year-round resort.

This revised edition of *Jasper Park Lodge* brings the reader up-to-date with these changes, and gives a glimpse ahead into the future. Susan Kavanagh, Director of Public Relations for the Lodge, and Edith Gourley of the Jasper-Yellowhead Historical Society, have been instrumental in helping me to revise the book.

Acknowledgements

Without a doubt, I couldn't have attempted this book without the tremendous help of Islay Cox. During her employment at Jasper Park Lodge as the public relations officer, Islay has collected many newsclippings, photographs, stories and reminiscences about the history of the Lodge. She spent many hours with me going through her material, introducing me to other staff and reviewing my manuscript. Her comments have been most helpful. Any errors in the book, however, remain the author's responsibility. Islay's constant encouragement and belief in the project were very appreciated — many thanks, Islay.

I also received a lot of encouragement from Mary Porter, of the Jasper-Yellowhead Historical Society. Mary suggested people to contact, retrieved material from the society archives for me, assisted with the selection of photographs for the book, and helped with its design and layout.

I would also like to thank Sam Wong, the General Manager of Jasper Park Lodge, for his enthusiasm in the project. Besides spending time with me discussing the management of the Lodge, Mr. Wong also allowed me complete access to staff and information.

Other people who were helpful in providing background information and checking stories were Mr. and Mrs. Jack Milligan, Bill Nicholl, Irma Schindler, and Doris Kensit.

The staff of many archives and libraries were most helpful and courteous, and gave me permission to reproduce photographs and other illustrations. Of particular note were Norman Lowe, historian for the Canadian National Railways in Montreal, and Connie Romani and Louise Verge at the CNR Photo Library there. All three gave me unlimited access to their collections. Thanks also to Don Bourden of the Archives of the Canadian Rockies in Banff, and the staff of the Glenbow-Alberta Institute Archives and Library in Calgary, Provincial Archives of Alberta in Edmonton, City of Edmonton Archives, Public Archives of Canada in Ottawa, and Provincial Archives of British Columbia in Victoria. Of course, thanks also to the Jasper-Yellowhead Historical Society for access to their collections, and for permission to reproduce their photographs.

And thank you, Ben Gadd, for your prompt and skillful editing of my manuscript.

Last, but not least, I would like to thank Jim and Julie Raynard, Walter and Meta McFarlane, and Elise Maltin, for providing a roof over my head and for lots of encouragement on my many trips to Jasper while working on this book.

Front cover: Reproduction of the cover of a 1926 CNR brochure. GLENBOW ARCHIVES.

Back cover: The lounge c. 1928. JASPER-YELLOWHEAD HISTORICAL SOCIETY.

Preface

There are two places from which to view Jasper Park Lodge. One is from afar, by riding the aerial tramway up The Whistlers. From the summit of the mountain the broad sweep of the Athabasca Valley lies at your feet. The jagged mountain ranges will first catch your eye, but it will eventually be drawn to the town in the centre of the valley, and to its surrounding lakes. There are Patricia and Pyramid, Edith and Annette, and the horseshoe shape of Lac Beauvert. And if you look closely you'll see the Lodge nestled in the trees on the shore of Lac Beauvert, although it blends in with its surroundings so well that it could easily be missed.

The other place is from the shore of Lac Beauvert, opposite the lodge. Above the lake lies the sleeping form of the "Old Man" of the Colin Range, staring skyward. If it's dusk, the lights of the lodge will be reflected in the water, and you may hear the strains of highland music as the piper announces the supper hour, or maybe you'll hear the wild cry of a loon.

I've enjoyed both views of Jasper Park Lodge many times since first coming to the park in 1974. That summer I worked in the office of the Canadian Imperial Bank of Commerce at the Lodge. The feeling of elegant history was everywhere, from the bars of the teller's window in the bank to the old cabins along the lakefront.

Despite the atmosphere, recording the history of Jasper Park Lodge was a difficult matter. The early records were lost in the fire in 1952, and many of the photographs and records in the head office in Montreal were also lost in another fire in the 1950s. My two main sources of information were the *Canadian National Railways Magazine* and the stories of people who remember JPL. Most of the early issues of the magazine contained articles or other references to Jasper Park Lodge and Jasper National Park. The difficulty with the personal stories was that there were so many! Thousands and thousands of guests and staff have stayed and worked at JPL, and a person could spend a lifetime collecting their anecdotes. I attempted to choose those accounts that would represent the life and labour of the Lodge.

Jasper National Park not only abounds with magnificent scenery and wildlife, but also has a rich history. I hope that this book will contribute in some small way to the recording and understanding of that history.

Contents

1 Grand Schemes for Grand Hotels

The letter was dated March 30, 1911 and was addressed to Frank Oliver, the minister of the interior for the Dominion government. In it, Chas. M. Hays, president of the Grand Trunk Pacific Railway (GTPR), requested " . . . the necessary land for the construction of hotels and hotel buildings, buildings for employees, stables, enclosures necessary for stock, etc., and also the exclusive privileges of constructing and operating hotels and of supplying transportation facilities for passengers through and over roads and trails in the Jasper Park Government Reserve."[1]

The request wasn't surprising, as the GTPR was nearly complete through Jasper Forest Park and the owners were eager to emulate the success of the Canadian Pacific Railway (CPR), which had luxury tourist accommodations at Banff, Lake Louise and Glacier House (Rogers Pass, British Columbia). The railway companies had realized that the provision of an adequate transportation system meant more than the mere operation of trains; it also meant the building of attractive hotels to encourage the public to use their railways.

Under the regime of Hays[2] the GTPR and Grand Trunk Railway (in eastern Canada) commenced work on what was intended to be an imposing chain of hotels across the continent. These included the Chateau Laurier, Fort Garry Hotel, Highland Inn and Camps, Minaki Lodge, and the Macdonald Hotel. There were also plans for hotels in Regina, Prince Rupert and Victoria. Major resort hotels in Jasper Park would be a crowning achievement.

The first accommodations in the park were private stopping places established during the construction days of the railway. Park superintendent McLaggan reported that by 1911 eight such places had been established, with "restaurant, sleeping and stable accommodation, there being room for eight hundred teams in these places."[3] By necessity these were rather crude places, and not meant to attract tourists.

The Dominion government recognized the future need for high-quality accommodation once the railway was complete, as there would then be easy access to the park for the first time. But the government was not

Hotel Fitzhugh was one of the earliest accommodations in Jasper. The name of the town was changed from Fitzhugh to Jasper in 1913. PUBLIC ARCHIVES CANADA PA20483

interested in granting the rights to only one company, as "it would hardly do to establish a park for the public benefit and then prevent any but one company from doing business in it." [4] Instead, a system had been set up by which sites for hotels would be granted under lease, a precedent which had been set in other parks.

Two years earlier, the GTPR had applied for the rights to the Miette Hot Springs, and a right-of-way between the springs and the railway line near the mouth of the Fiddle River, the latter to be used for "pipe line, drive way, steam or electric railway." [5] That request had been firmly rejected by the government, perhaps based upon the success of the government-controlled hot springs at Banff. The Miette Hot Springs are the hottest in the Canadian Rockies, and the government wasn't about to give them away.

In the same letter in 1911 Mr. Hays requested 2-4 ha (5-10 acres) of land at some as yet undetermined point between Brûlé Lake and Jasper Lake, for a proposed hotel called "Château Miette." The exact location for the hotel was determined in July of 1911 by A. O. Wheeler. Wheeler was the president of the new Alpine Club of Canada and a successful topographical surveyor. The GTPR asked Wheeler to map the Jasper Park and Mt. Robson regions during the club's 1911 expedition to Mt. Robson, and to report on possible sites for hotels, chalets and trails.

Accompanied by Chief Superintendent Howard Douglas, and various railway officials — H. R. Charlton, general advertising agent; W. P. Hinton, general passenger agent; and R. C. W. Lett, travelling passenger and colonization agent — Wheeler spent three days near Brûlé Lake inspecting sites for a hotel. A site was chosen on the east side of Fiddle River, about half a kilometre (a quarter of a mile) from the canyon and 2½ km (1½ miles) south of the railway line, on a bench about 60 m (200 feet) above the valley bottom. Wheeler was very enthusiastic about the site, insisting that " . . . there is little doubt but that Château Miette will be a great favorite both as a recreation and health resort, for, doubtless, the water from Miette Hot Springs, which are said to be on a par with those at Banff, will be piped down the canyon for use at the hotel."[6]

Wheeler was also strongly in favour of opening up the Mt. Robson area. He suggested that the railway should build a pony trail past Kinney Lake to Berg Lake, and build a chalet at Berg Lake itself. The GTPR was already intending to build a hotel near the junction of the Robson River with the Fraser River.

The Dominion government first investigated whether the Château Miette proposal would interfere with the new Canadian Northern Railway's plans in the park. But there was no problem, as the tracks for the other railway would run on the opposite side of the Athabasca River. The government then expressed keen interest in the proposal. The commissioner of parks requested that his chief superintendent in Edmonton investigate connecting the springs to the railway line near the hotel with a monorail. Although photographs and plans of a prototype in use near Calgary were obtained, the project never materialized.

The railway had requested a lease of 22 ha (55 acres): 20 for the actual site of the hotel, and 2 ha to enclose "Bear Trail Springs" nearby, which would be the source of their water. The architect's drawing showed a beautiful arched structure built around three sides of a central garden, complete with a fountain in the middle. It was ornate and luxurious. It would cost about half a million dollars to build and was designed such that it could easily be extended in the future. By 1912 the company had the plans drawn and were only waiting for a lease before beginning construction.

The proposed lease was for 42 years, with renewal subject to conditions that would protect the park and the general public. The chief superintendent of the Dominion Parks Branch even recommended that an additional area be set aside for the company to develop a golf course. The suggested rent was $500 per year, based on the rent paid by the Canadian Pacific Railway for their Banff Springs Hotel (roughly $4 per ha or $10 per acre). Although the railway was eager to begin construction (their line through the park was completed in 1912), and park officials seemed to favour the proposal, the Dominion government delayed granting the lease. The delay was caused in part by questions concerning school lands and which government department had jurisdiction over water within the park.

Meanwhile the railway continued to develop plans for other hotels. In the spring of 1913 they applied for two leases in the vicinity of the town of Fitzhugh (the name was changed to Jasper later that year). One was a two-hectare (five-acre) lease at the site of their engineer's camp, locally known as "Snape's Hill," and adjoining land in the immediate vicinity for golf and recreation grounds. This site was at the south end of town, near Cabin Creek. The next year Sir Arthur Conan Doyle gave "his assistance and practical knowledge" to the laying out of a nine-hole golf course at the

The Grand Trunk Pacific Railway had planned to build an elaborate hotel, Château Miette, along the Fiddle River in the eastern part of the park.
PUBLIC ARCHIVES CANADA NL13574

The Jasper Park Hotel, to be built on the western edge of town, never materialized.
GLENBOW ARCHIVES

site.[7] The second lease was for 40 ha (100 acres) on the south shore of Pyramid Lake, a few kilometres north of the townsite.

Soon, though, the company was in financial difficulty, and by 1914 barely had enough funds to complete the main line to the coast, let alone three grand hotels. Ironically, the Dominion government was finally ready to grant the lease for Château Miette and was suddenly feeling public pressure for accommodations. By February, 1915, the government was so desperate that they were asking the railway to at least construct cheap log buildings at the three sites. The department was willing to "not be too stringent in regard to the appearance of the buildings and would be prepared to deal generously in the matter of temporary sites" and even to "be disposed to deal reasonably with anyone else who might apply for rights in this connection."[8]

Thus, the GTPR's grand plans were put on the shelf[9], and Tent City came into being.

2 Tent City

The driving force behind the railway's continued involvement in tourist lodgings in the park was Mr. R. C. W. Lett, a tourist agent for the GTPR in Edmonton. He recognized the potential of the 1915 World's Fair in San Francisco as a way to induce travellers to visit Canada, and particularly Jasper, on their way to and from the spectacle. His enthusiasm, plus the pressure from the government to follow up on their hotel proposals, prompted the railway company to approach Mr. Robert Kenneth, of the Edmonton Tent and Mattress Company.[1] Mr. Kenneth was also impressed by the possibilities for tourism in Jasper Park.

Robert Kenneth. PROVINCIAL ARCHIVES OF ALBERTA: E. BROWN B7637

6

The GTPR sent one of its Edmonton employees, Mr. H. R. Tilley, to Jasper to investigate locations that would be suitable for a temporary tourist camp. Accompanied by Fred and Jack Brewster[2], pioneer outfitters in the region, he visited Lake Edith, Pyramid Lake and other potential sites. Finally the Brewsters showed him their own personal preference, Lac Beauvert, which at that time was called "Horseshoe Lake" because of its shape.

The location was ideal. From the shores of the lake one could see The Whistlers, Signal Mountain, Pyramid Mountain, the peaks of the Colin Range — most prominent of which was Roche Bonhomme, the "Old Man" — and the impressive peak that was later named Mt. Edith Cavell. The Athabasca River flowed nearby, and there was already a log suspension bridge built across it in 1913, near Old Fort Point.

The road snaked right past Lac Beauvert to Maligne Canyon, which was fast becoming a very popular tourist destination. Upon seeing Maligne Canyon one traveller remarked that "any other canyon is like a crack in a teacup."

With the help of Fred and Jack Brewster, Robert Kenneth constructed Jasper Park Camp on the shore of Lac Beauvert. The railway ran the following publicity announcement in their Passenger Department Bulletin:

> During the coming summer, Jasper, Alta. is expected to become the central and popular resort in the wonderful Jasper Park, on the line of the Grand Trunk Pacific in the Canadian Rockies. A large number of Transcontinental passengers who are lovers of nature will desire to stop off in the Mountain fastnesses of the Canadian Rockies and enjoy the superb Mountain scenery and bracing air that is found in this locality.
>
> Preparatory to the building of the proposed Grand Trunk Pacific hotels in the Mountain territory, accommodation this year will be provided by the erection of a tent city. The sleeping tents will contain board floors and will be equipped and furnished with comfortable beds and all the accessories that go to make up a modern bedroom. A large marquee will be erected for dining accommodation and the entire camp will be under capable management.[3]

There were ten large tents, each with wooden floors and walls. The main dining tent served as a lounge in the evenings, where guests visited, read and played bridge. Kenneth managed the camp; he hired a competent chef, waitresses and housekeepers to take charge of dining room and domestic arrangements.

The inclusive rates at the camp were $2.50 and $3 per day and $15 and $18 per week. There was a $1 charge for the round trip from the railway station in Brewster Brothers' horsedrawn carriages. Hand baggage went free. The GTPR offered a special round-trip ticket from Edmonton, good for two weeks, for only $8.45. Kenneth also advertised fishing, mountain climbing, boating, and canoeing, the latter with "no mud."

Tent City, as the lodging was commonly called, opened on June 15, 1915.[4] Three days before the opening the following people were registered as the first guests: E. V. Leland of Cambridge, Massachusetts; G. P. Ireland

Tent City ca. 1915. JASPER-YELLOWHEAD HISTORICAL SOCIETY

A group of newspaper people at the opening of Tent City. PUBLIC ARCHIVES CANADA PA11271

of Springfield, Mass.; Martin W. Luse, of Harrisburg, Pennsylvania; and J. E. Bell of Seattle. On opening day Mr. and Mrs. A. O. Merrick of Winnipeg, Mary S. Webster of Toronto, F. M. Olsen of Edmonton, T. Thorvaldsen and L. L. Burgess of Saskatoon, the Chowns of Kingston, Ontario, Mr. and Mrs. Armstrong from Ottawa, and G. D. Davidson of Calgary were also registered. These people may have been part of a Canadian press excursion. Other guests that summer were James Lightbody, a public relations official with the British Columbia Electric Railway Company, and Miss Josephine Adams Rathbone, chief librarian of the Pratt Institute, New York City.

Ten days after the opening of Tent City, W. H. "Billy" Robinson, later head of the Canadian National Railways photographic services, arrived, beginning a long career of making still pictures and movies of Jasper. His work and enthusiasm were instrumental in publicizing the park throughout the world.

The first season went well, with over 260 visitors registering from across Canada, throughout the United States and abroad. Much of the success stemmed from the heavy advertising that was done by the railway.

Naomi Radford, from Edmonton, who had stayed at Tent City as a child, recalled collecting pine and fir cones and selling them to the American tourists for 5¢ apiece. When her father found out, however, he made her return the money!

Despite its success, Tent City closed immediately following its first season: a world war was imminent. The camp didn't reopen until 1919. In

*In 1919 Jack and Fred Brewster bought
Tent City from Robert Kenneth.*
VANCOUVER CITY ARCHIVES

that year (on June 5) Jack Brewster, along with his brother Fred, now a
major returned from war service, bought Tent City from Robert Kenneth.

Tent City continued to be very popular. In his 1919 annual report, park
superintendent Rogers reported that "the park was crowded beyond capaci-
ty of accommodation all through the past season, and the want of a suitable
and modern hotel is a serious handicap. The 'Tent City', with accommodation for sixty guests, were compelled to put out the 'no accommodation'
sign nearly every train day."[5]

In 1920 the Brewsters built a log kitchen and dining room. They also
built a cabin for their own use across the road from the camp. A newly-built
dance pavilion, with tiered seats, extended over the lake, and an orchestra
of volunteer musicians frequently played. There was even a quoits pitch (a
popular game at the time, similar to horseshoes). One lady from New York
brought an organ and stored it in the cabin, bringing it out on the grass
every Sunday for religious services.

But change was on the horizon. Most of the railways across the
country were in financial difficulties. By 1916 and 1917 the Canadian
Northern Railway and the GTPR were amalgamating their lines in an
attempt to stay solvent. As a result, the Canadian National Railways
Company was formed to join them all into a national system.[6] The new
railway was also interested in tourist accommodations, and it had the
money and backing to pursue its ideas.

Fred and Jack Brewster used to camp at Lac Beauvert long before Tent
City was built and had always dreamed of a major hotel there. Their dream
was about to come true.

3 A Wilderness Retreat is Built

In 1921 the newly formed Canadian National Railways took over Tent City. They immediately upgraded the tent camp to eight temporary log bungalows, and "Jasper Park Lodge" opened in June, 1922.

The new accommodations consisted of about a dozen log bungalows, each with four bedrooms and a lounge. There were also a main dining hall with connecting dance pavilion, management office and kitchen, and a central lounge, complete with animal heads, a great stone fireplace and gramophones. Some 65 guests could be put up, but the dining hall could serve more, for the Lodge was encouraging visitors to pitch tents on the site of the old Tent City.

The buildings were completed in less than two months under the supervision of A. S. McLean, western superintendent of the CNR's hotel department. The actual work was coordinated by C. M. Lang, engineer in charge of CNR construction.

· There were several railway officials on hand at the opening ceremonies: W. E. Duperow, general passenger agent in Winnipeg and Osborne Scott, general passenger agent in Vancouver, among others. Scott had been with the Canadian Northern Railway[1] and was a great supporter of Jasper National Park, having traversed many of its trails on foot and by horse. There were many visitors registering from the United States. A large number of newspapers from across western Canada sent representatives: the Victoria *Times*, Victoria *Colonist*, Vancouver *Province*, Vancouver *Sun*, Vancouver *World*, Edmonton *Journal*, Edmonton *Bulletin*, Calgary *Herald*, Winnipeg *Free Press* and Winnipeg *Tribune*. In late June a party of Rotarians stayed at the Lodge on their way to a convention in Los Angeles. They travelled by special train through the Rockies to Prince Rupert, where they caught a boat down the Inside Passage to Vancouver.

Under the direction of Sir Henry Thornton, the first president of the new railway, the hotel system was expanded. On his first western tour in January 1923, Thornton visited Jasper Park Lodge. He looked at the site of the new bungalow resort with the "eye of the passenger man who is always on the alert for subsidiary attractions with which to augment his revenues."[2] Sir Henry's concept of the function of the CNR hotel system was that the hotels should attract tourists to Canada, which would swell railway

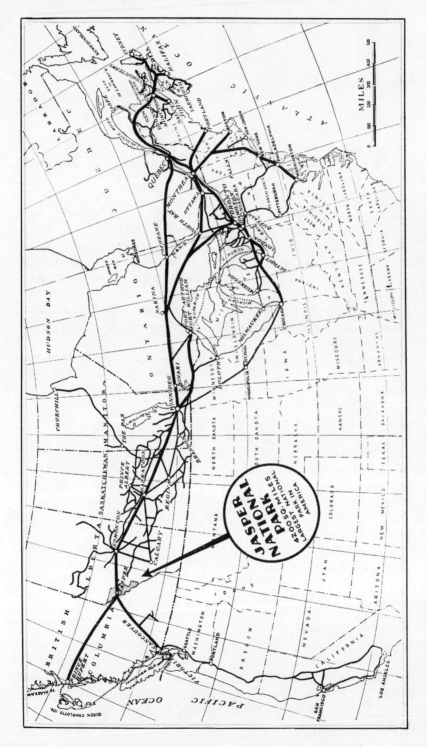

Jasper National Park was a heavily advertised highlight of the Canadian National Railways system. CANADIAN NATIONAL

operating revenues, increase the volume of money in circulation through local businesses, and best of all, add to net profits because the money stayed in the country. With his continental tastes and experiences, Thornton imported well-known international chefs, and the food of the CN hotels became known far and wide. Thornton was the untiring, driving force behind the railway in its early years and he expected just as much from his employees as from himself.

Sir Henry was frequently called upon to entertain prominent patrons. These included many millionaires who thronged to JPL in the summer and expected something special for their money. After hobnobbing with such a character they often extended their stay and considered their money well spent. He greatly enjoyed riding, and was fondly referred to as "the big man on the big horse." There was always a horse waiting for him on his arrival at the station.

Sir Henry Thornton, the first president of the Canadian National Railways, was known as "the big man on the big horse." JASPER PARK LODGE

The credit for the overall design of Jasper Park Lodge was generally given to John Schofield, once chief architect for Trans-Canada Air Lines, and later for the CNR system. Schofield maintained, though, that the credit for the idea of a bungalow-style resort was not just his alone, but seemed to come to life spontaneously from different sources. A cluster of moderate-sized buildings and cabins seemed better-suited to the lakeshore site and the surrounding wide valley than a massive hotel would be.

On a July day in 1920 a young Englishman by the name of Godfrey

Jasper Park Lodge was designed as a bungalow resort because it was felt that a massive hotel would not be suited to the surroundings. CANADIAN NATIONAL

The central building, built in the winter of 1922-23, and later enlarged, was touted as the largest single-storey log building in the world. PROVINCIAL ARCHIVES OF ALBERTA A1485

Milnes walked into Schofield's Toronto office. After being badly wounded in the war he had immigrated to Canada, looking for a fresh start. By the time that he visited Schofield, he was disheartened by the seeming lack of opportunity for his talents in his new home. Schofield was sympathetic, most impressed by the samples of Milnes' work, and he hired him as a draughtsman immediately. One day Schofield called Milnes in on a Saturday afternoon and outlined his plans for the new Lodge — he also said that he needed the plans in a hurry. Milnes finished his drawings that afternoon.

The central building and the surrounding bungalows were built during the winter of 1922–23. They were constructed in the winter, when the wood was comparatively sapless and dry, and it was easy to haul the logs over the snow. Initially, trees cleared from the site were used in construction, but eventually logs were hauled in from near Maligne Canyon. This was accomplished by Fred and Jack Brewster, using sleighs during the winter. On the site the logs were piled together, four-square, while the cracks between were chinked with a mixture of moss, sawdust and cement. If the logs had shrunk at all by the following year, a preparation of creosote was injected, making the building snug. Planed lumber for the hardwood floor and trimmings was shipped in by train. Local stone was used for the pillars and fireplace. Western red cedar for upright pillars and the shake roof was brought in from British Columbia.

John Craig, the CNR's building superintendent from Winnipeg, supervised the construction. A lot of Jasper men worked on the site. They used to walk over and they made a shortcut by dropping a tree across the river at the closest place, thereby cutting the walking time in half. They were augmented by a large crew brought in by train. Ralph James, a rancher and outfitter from Pocahontas (a tiny coal-mining community near the park's east gate, now abandoned), carved the fancy woodwork inside the main lodge.

The main building had cost $461,000 to construct and was touted as the largest single-storey log structure in the world. It included lounges, a dining room, snack room, kitchen and administrative offices. The business offices, card rooms, telephones and telegraph, reservations and ticket desks, transportation desk, newsstand, shops, hairdressing and manicure salons, and information bureau were in one wing of the building. The main lounge was the pride of the building and well-known for its specially-designed wicker furniture, magnificent stone fireplace and mounted animal heads. The lounge was very spacious, but the furniture arrangement was such that there was a feeling of smaller, separate spaces for visiting, playing cards, reading, or writing letters.

In 1927–28 the lodge was greatly enlarged: the rotunda was extended, doubling its size, a dancing and convention hall was built off the rotunda, and a bedroom wing was added. The bedrooms led off the central corridor, whose outer doors led directly outside onto gravel paths.

The central lounge was an elaborate affair, well-known for its magnificent stone fireplace, trophy heads and specially-designed wicker furniture.
JASPER PARK LODGE

Three hundred people could dance comfortably in the ballroom at one time.
CANADIAN NATIONAL

Hostesses escorted guests to bridge tables and dances in the ballroom, entering through the lounge. The orchestra played in the ballroom every evening for dining and dancing, except for Sunday nights when there was a concert. Three hundred people could dance comfortably at one time. The ballroom also served for showing movies, and with the use of a folding partition, large conventions could be held. Doors also opened off the lounge onto the patio, and thus to the snack room. Guests entered the main dining room, which could handle 400 people at one sitting, through a heart-shaped grille. Tea was served each afternoon on the veranda of the lodge — a tradition which is still maintained.

The general effect of the main lodge was that it was "snug as a 'den' and as spacious as the state-room in some great castle."[3]

The bungalow "village" followed the curve of the lake. It had miniature paved streets, complete with lamps and gardens. The old-English lantern of wrought iron was adopted as the official symbol of Jasper Park Lodge. Such lanterns had always evoked an air of sentiment, with their pleasant suggestion of comfort, rest and jollity. The lanterns hung at the train station and at each bungalow door, lighted the path to the lodge and were seen on signboards along the road.

The bungalows ranged in size from four to over twenty rooms. They were centrally-heated and each one had a sitting room with writing desk,

The orchestra played every evening for dining and dancing, ca. 1937.
CANADIAN NATIONAL

The spacious veranda was a place for relaxing and visiting. JASPER PARK LODGE

The main reception area featured the reservations desk, transportation desk and curio shop.
CANADIAN NATIONAL

The bungalows were built along miniature streets, ca. 1927. JASPER PARK LODGE

bedrooms with private baths, hot and cold water, electric lights and telephones. Guests were greeted with a flower display outside and cut flowers inside. Including the bungalows and the few rooms in the lodge, there was accommodations for 425 guests in 1927. American Plan rates, with meals included, varied from $7.50 to $40.00. There was a 10% discount for stays of a month or more.

The Lodge had its own fleet of cars for picking up guests at the railway station. During 1926 a total of 15,336 passengers were transported to and from the station, and more than 3000 visitors enjoyed the scenic drive to Mt. Edith Cavell. Almost 25,000 pieces of baggage were handled by hotel porters. A Canadian government customs officer was stationed at the Lodge so that guests arriving from out of the country with bonded baggage could have it examined at leisure.

The road from Jasper to the Lodge and the Lodge "streets" themselves were paved in 1927 in an experiment using bituminous sand from Fort McMurray, in northern Alberta. The summer traffic was quite heavy on that road, with at times the equivalent of 500 cars per day, including a fleet of two-ton trucks operated by the railway.

The late 1920s saw yet more construction: an outdoor swimming pool in 1926, the power house and laundry on Mildred Lake in 1927, Point Cabin in 1928, the golf clubhouse and greenhouses in 1929, and Outlook Cabin in 1930. Point and Outlook were two luxurious cabins that had their own kitchens, dining rooms and servants' quarters. New buildings for the 1930 season included two 10-room cabins, one 8-room cabin, one 16-room

Attention to small details was evident throughout the Lodge, as shown by this carved chair. CANADIAN NATIONAL

The mailbox was created from a beaver-gnawed stump.
CANADIAN NATIONAL

The Lodge's own fleet of cars picked passengers up at the railway station.
CANADIAN NATIONAL

This sign was at the end of the railway station platform. JASPER-YELLOWHEAD HISTORICAL SOCIETY

cabin, one 2-suite cabin, a 23-bedroom building near the clubhouse for golfers, two new staff cabins and a first-aid building. Other changes that year were enlarged dining rooms, a service station and garage with new buses and cars, an enlarged curio shop, a new specialty gift shop, and enclosed verandas on some cabins. Accommodations increased to 550 people.

The curio shop had been opened by Frank Slark, a photographer from

Luxurious Point Cabin was built in 1928, and had its own kitchen, dining room and servants' quarters. CANADIAN NATIONAL

Lady Thornton personally chose the furnishings for Outlook Cabin.
CANADIAN NATIONAL

A secluded alcove in the upstairs of Point Cabin was suitable for reading, writing or a quiet game of cards. CANADIAN NATIONAL

The old stone garage housed the Lodge's fleet of cars. PARKS CANADA

Victoria. He had heard of the CNR's purchase of Jasper Park Camp in 1921, and foresaw great possibilities. He spent three months photographing in the park, and presented his collection to the railway officials, who were very pleased with his work. Slark then applied for and obtained a concession in the lodge, on a percentage basis. This concession, the first at the Lodge,

Macleans, 1 May 1934. PUBLIC ARCHIVES CANADA NL8133

was in a corner of the lounge, and Slark sold photographs (in both black-and-white and sepia tone), postcards, curios, Indian handcrafts, souvenirs and boxed chocolates. Two years later a separate octagonal building was set up as a curio shop, with photographic facilities in the basement. In August of 1927 Mr. Slark died while mountain climbing in the Tonquin Valley.[4] Over the years many other local businessmen have held concessions at JPL.

In 1931, during royal commission hearings on transportation in Canada, it was felt that the criteria of public expenditures for the railways must not only be to operate at a profit, but to make contributions to the community also. Although the CNR's Jasper Park expenditures had totalled $2,576,-744, Thornton maintained that railway revenues directly attributable to JPL had paid for the capital investment, plus $800,000.[5] Tourist traffic was becoming very important in western Canada.

Tourism in Jasper National Park took a giant leap from 1939 to 1940. In 1939, 3100 automobiles and approximately 21,000 persons were recorded as entering the park, but the figures jumped enormously to more than 19,000 cars and 83,000 people in 1940. Most of the increase was credited to the opening of the Banff-Jasper Highway (now the Icefields Parkway).

The gateway to Jasper Park Lodge frames Mt. Edith Cavell in the distance.
CANADIAN NATIONAL

The Lodge was closed from the fall of 1942 until the spring of 1946 due to the war. The management of the CN hotel department stated that the decision was made "as a result of a careful study of Canada's wartime economy, including manpower, foodstuffs and transportation" to enable their temporary help, numbering several hundred people, to be "available for service on farms or in munitions plants in their home communities."[6] Also, international tourism was at a low ebb in those years.

During the winter of 1943-44 the Lodge was used as a base for the winter training of the Lovat Scouts, a Scottish regiment being trained as special mountain troops. Their training had begun in Scotland and Wales, and was completed in Jasper. Jasper Park Lodge was requisitioned by the army as their headquarters, and Colonel Harcourt, a Canadian Royal Engineer officer, was in charge of winterizing the buildings. The troops arrived in December and occupied camps at Maligne Lake, in the Columbia Icefield area, in Tonquin Valley and at Mt. Edith Cavell.

Jasper Park Lodge was the headquarters for the Lovat Scouts, a Scottish regiment being trained as special mountain troops, during the winter of 1943-44.
JASPER-YELLOWHEAD HISTORICAL SOCIETY

Most of the original log bungalows were replaced between the late 1940s and early 1960s in a modernization program. They were designed to complement the new lodge built in 1953, but to still blend in with the natural surroundings. Nine of the original bungalows, including Point and Outlook cabins, are still in use and very popular with guests.

4   A Night of Ruin

Disaster struck Jasper Park Lodge at the height of the summer season in 1952: the large central lodge building was completely destroyed by fire. As one newspaper reported it, ''a fire at any time of year is usually disastrous, but in a summer resort at the peak of the tourist season it is more than that. It is a calamity which affects the lives of thousands of people.''[1]

With patience, resourcefulness and good humour, on the part of both guests and staff, the resort operated through to the end of the season. Some guests did cancel their reservations when informed that they might have had to face inconveniences. Others persevered. The staff managed to maintain a level of service such that there was only a 25% decrease in the number of guests over the previous season.

The fire was discovered shortly after nine o'clock in the evening, on

On the night of July 15, 1952, the central building burned to the ground. Through the efforts of many volunteer firefighters all of the other buildings were saved.
JASPER-YELLOWHEAD HISTORICAL SOCIETY

Tuesday, July 15th. There were about 580 guests registered at the time. An employee discovered the fire when he opened a cloakroom door. Although two bellmen attempted to contain the blaze with fire extinguishers the flames immediately roared into the main part of the building. A guest ran into the ballroom, where a dozen couples were dancing, and yelled "Fire!" only seconds before the guests and musicians saw flames advancing rapidly along the varnished floor. Other guests were in front of the great fireplace in the main hall, playing cards. Hazel Hickey remembered fleeing from the bridge table, only to run back to retrieve her mink coat from the back of her chair.

To help in keeping people calm, Len Hopkins and his band continued playing "Pittsburgh, Pennsylvania" as the dance crowd left in an orderly fashion. They then fled with their instruments, but the fire spread so quickly that they lost their music and instrument cases. A blind man was led to safety by two employees. The shellacked timbers and floors burned like tinder, balls of fire raced along the ceiling and the curtains stood straight out due to the draft. The many exits were a tremendous advantage in ensuring that everyone was evacuated quickly. There were no injuries among the guests.

The aid of the town fire department, run by the park administration and assisted by volunteers, was delayed until a forest fire lookout man on Signal Mountain reported the fire, because the telephone lines from the Lodge to town were burnt out (there is now a direct alarm connection). Initially the lookout man was told that everything was okay; that the Lodge had a permit to burn brush. A few minutes later he called again, insisting that it was no brush fire, as the flames were reflected in his windows. Within an hour of the fire starting, all four of the lookouts in the valley had reported the blaze. Hundreds of townspeople watched the horrifying spectacle from Pyramid Lake, Pyramid Mountain, the opposite side of Lac Beauvert and other vantage points.

The guests, staff members and the Lodge's own fire brigade were aided in their attempts to stop the fire by the Jasper volunteer fire brigade, the park warden service, the Royal Canadian Mounted Police, Canadian army personnel in the area, and Comstock Midwestern pipeline workers. As there was no hope in saving the main building, efforts were concentrated on protecting the nearby cabins and the golf clubhouse. Luckily a light wind blew the flames toward the lake and away from the threatened bungalows. Water from the pool and the lake was used to combat the fire.

At times bursts of flames threatened to spread to pine and Douglas-fir trees near the building. Some trees between the lodge and the cabins were cut down. At about eleven o'clock, just when the flames seemed to be losing strength, an ammonia tank in the lodge basement blew, causing another flare-up. It was eventually contained. Some of the employees donned gas respirators and attempted to salvage the stores, but to no avail. One young lad, not knowing how to properly operate his respirator, nearly suffocated and was dragged to safety by his companions. Around midnight the roof collapsed with a roar.

The hotel staff responded remarkably: wrapped in wet blankets and towels they lay on tinder-dry cabin roofs, dousing sparks with fire extinguishers, soaking the clothes of the firefighters, and starting a coffee and sandwich brigade for them.

One employee, Len Peters, secretary to the general manager, received severe face and head burns. About ten volunteers also were burned, but less seriously. Everyone credited Peters with saving the lives of many of the guests by marshalling them towards the exits. Mr. Peters was rushed to Jasper's small hospital for treatment, but early the next morning he was flown to the University of Alberta hospital in Edmonton by an Associated Airways plane. Mr. Peters died in Edmonton as a result of his burns.

Robert Sommerville, superintendent of the CN's hotel department, had just arrived at the Lodge that afternoon for a periodical visit. He praised the actions of Mr. Peters:

> He paid the supreme sacrifice in a display of valour and courage beyond the call of duty. Mr. Peters was engaged in fighting the fire inside the building with a fire extinguisher. He entered one of the burning offices, hoping to get at the seat of the blaze but was cut off by flames and received such serious burns that he died a few days later. Mr. Peters' courageous actions were entirely in keeping with his sense of duty and will be remembered by all who were there.[2]

All of the guests were evacuated from their cabins, some of which were within ten metres of the blazing inferno. Most were able to return to their cabins after the fire was brought under control. Those that had been staying in the lodge itself were housed by the townspeople, and 20 spent the night on a sleeping car at the station.

By 7:00 the morning after the fire, the kitchen and dining room staff were ready to serve a cafeteria-style breakfast to some 1200 guests, staff and firefighters. Temporary kitchen and dining room facilities were set up in the staff dining hall. Food was procured from town during the night, even while the fire raged. By mid-afternoon adequate food supplies had arrived from Edmonton. Special dining and cafe-car equipment had been brought in as a precaution, but was never used.

Sommerville recalled the chaos after the fire, and how everyone responded to the emergency with good cheer:

> We were in a real predicament. The house was full, but all the ledgers had burned up. We didn't know who our guests were, how much they owed us, how long they had been there or how we were going to feed them. We gave them breakfast in the staff cafeteria: one egg, a slice of toast and a bit of bacon on a paper plate, with coffee, tea or milk on the side. Some of the fussiest people on the continent, who would normally have raised the roof at any imperfection in service, were the cheeriest of all when the chips were down. By noon, we were feeding guests in the golf clubhouse, where we have a small kitchen. By night, we had brought in china and silverware from the Macdonald, in Edmonton, one of our chain of hotels. We brought in a special train in case anybody wanted to leave, but not more than fifty people got on, among

them a few who simply skipped out on their bills. The rest stuck tight. The guests came in and recalled, as best they could, what they owed us. They didn't even forget the incidentals, such as room service and long-distance-phone charges.[3]

Although the railway had three special trains sent out to transport guests who wanted to leave, only 26 elected to do so. Through it all the guests took the inconveniences in good part, except one wealthy dowager who complained, "but I'm not used to carrying a tray." Hildebrandt, the suave maître d', haughtily drew himself up. "Madam," he replied, "neither am I!"[4]

Within a few hours, conveniences such as the beauty salon, barber shop and valet service were set up. The staff recreation hall became a lounge and ballroom for guests, with dance music nightly by Len Hopkins and his orchestra. The loss of the switchboard in the main building meant that telephone services were cut off until a new switchboard was flown in from Dawson Creek, British Columbia.

The lounge of the golf clubhouse temporarily became the front office and administrative quarters. Bill Nicholl, the head gardener, was asked to put in a rock garden to beautify the entrance to this temporary office. This was at three o'clock on Friday afternoon, three days after the fire. In about 20 minutes a truckload of rocks, earth and geraniums were on hand, and by six o'clock Mr. Nicholl and his helpers had completed a rock garden that looked as if it had been planted at the beginning of the season.

The day after the fire. JASPER PARK LODGE

The construction of a new lodge began almost immediately after the fire.
PCL CONSTRUCTION GROUP: HARRY ROWED PHOTO

There were few standing structures left of the main lodge after the fire. All that remained were part of the "Tavern Room" overlooking the lake, the rock garden out front, the towering stone chimney and fireplace, two blackened lampposts, a stone patio and two stone columns, and a few of the log columns, partly burned, that had marked the main entrance.

Defective wiring in the cloakroom was the apparent cause of the inferno; rumours of a smouldering cigarette left by a careless bellboy were dismissed. The loss was over a million dollars, which was covered by the railway's own insurance company. It was also rumoured that nearly $60,000 in cash and $4000 in stamps in the Lodge office were lost, but the story was never confirmed.

Within a few days of the fire, construction began on a temporary dining facility for staff since the original mess hall was being used to feed the guests.

The rough plans for the lodge itself were already drawn, as Sommerville had always felt that the old building might burn down someday, being built of wood. By the end of August the excavation for the building was completed. Poole Construction Company, of Edmonton, were hired as the general contractors. By September 20 they began pouring concrete for foundations and ground-floor slabs. The first structural steel was erected in early November. While the good weather held, 160 men were rushing to do as much as possible. Stonemasons were even flown in from Britain and Italy due to a shortage of skilled Canadians. The roof was completed before the cold weather set in. Nearly 400 men worked on the lodge all winter, finishing the work on June 9, 1953, the day before a large convention was due to arrive.

The new lodge was constructed of fireproof steel, concrete and fieldstone, with a cedar roof. Skillful architecture, reminiscent of the work of Frank Lloyd Wright, ensured that the building blended in well with both the natural surroundings and the original bungalows. The design was based on four wings containing an open lounge with a large double fireplace, dining rooms and kitchens, ballroom, front office, administration offices, shops, transportation reservation desk, snack room and cocktail lounge.

The new lodge was also designed to blend in well with its surroundings. The old pool and boathouse were replaced later. CANADIAN NATIONAL

For the first time there was a second storey, which included some guest rooms.

The two totem poles marking the stairway to the lower level of the lodge were carved by Canadian sculptor Arthur Price, from the Ottawa area. They carry on the tradition started by an early GTPR vice-president who brought the original Raven Totem to Jasper. (A concrete replica stands by the train station.)

The cost of the new building was roughly $3 million. It covered an area of about 7000 square metres (75,000 square feet), or about ¾ of a hectare (1¾ acres). When it opened on June 10, there were some 12,000 advance bookings. Every visitor had become an advertiser.

At the time that the lodge burned down, Fred Brewster was up at Maligne Lake with a group of sightseers. Somehow word got to him in the middle of the night, and he set out immediately, arriving in the morning light. He uttered only one sentence when he viewed the charred ruins: "I'm glad my brother Jack wasn't here [to see this]." Jack had passed away the previous year.

There were three main factors that allowed the night, and the season, to be salvaged: the ability of the Lodge staff to act on their own initiative and as a team during the emergency; the ability of the railway to marshall its resources at a moment's notice, and the way in which the townspeople rallied to help.

The courage and ingenuity of the employees became a world-wide press story. It's possible that it was this type of dedication that played a part in President Gordon's decision to repair the damage immediately, and while doing so to upgrade Jasper Park Lodge to a world-class modern resort.

5 Royalty and Movie Stars

Jasper Park Lodge attracts a diverse clientele, not just the "newlyweds or nearly deads," as the saying goes. They've hailed from almost every country in the world and from virtually every occupation in life. But JPL has been home to its share of famous people: writers, artists, royalty, Hollywood stars and the rich of the world.

A partial list of the elite is impressive. There are movie stars Bing Crosby, Marilyn Monroe and Dinah Shore; governors-general Montgomery, Byng, Bessborough; prime ministers MacKenzie King, Trudeau, Clark; writers such as Sir Arthur Conan Doyle, Bob Davis, Courtney Ryley Cooper, Norman Reilly Raine (a well-known Toronto newspaperman); John Fisher (Canadian radio and TV commentator); Sir Frederick Banting (co-discoverer of insulin); Chief Justice Hughes of the U.S. Supreme Court; King George VI and Queen Elizabeth; the Duke of Kent; Thomas W. Mitchell, A. Y. Jackson and Franklin Carmichael (all artists from the Group of Seven); Judge Buffington of Philadelphia (he used to leave bottles floating on the lake, each containing a message); Alexander Bajkov (former keeper of the Czar of Russia's fishing preserves); baseball great Joe DiMaggio; and members of such famous families as the Curtises, Colgates, Kennedys and Rockefellers.

Sir Arthur Conan Doyle and Lady Doyle first visited the park in 1914. While here he wrote "The Athabaska Trail," a poem about the packhorse and packer. During his second visit to Jasper in 1923, Sir Arthur wrote the following in the Lodge's visitors' book:

> An adaptation of an ancient story occurs to me. A New York man reached Heaven, and as he passed the gate, Peter said, "I am sure you will like it." A Pittsburgh man followed, and Peter said, "It will be a very great change for you." Finally there came a man from Jasper Park. "I am afraid," said Peter, "that you will be disappointed."[1]

During their cross-Canada tour in 1939 King George VI and Queen Elizabeth stayed at Jasper Park Lodge. They arrived from Vancouver on Thursday, June 1, and departed the following day. Although their time was short, and actively spent, the royal couple considered their stay very relaxing in the midst of a gruelling round of public appearances.

When the Queen arrived at Outlook Cabin she was very impressed

King George VI and Queen Elizabeth stayed in Outlook Cabin in 1939.
JASPER-YELLOWHEAD HISTORICAL SOCIETY

with it, and checked the cabin over thoroughly. "She poked about the cupboards, the electric warming oven, the electric refrigerator and gave the rugs, curtains [and] drapes close scrutiny."[2] She also noticed that the golden dinner service used by them at the Chateau Laurier, in Ottawa, had been brought to the Lodge for their use.

Within half an hour of arrival, Their Majesties were off to Maligne Canyon, where the King took many feet of movie film, and the Queen kept up a running conversation with Major James Wood, park superintendent, about the wildflowers. After lunch back at their cabin, they were off to Mt. Edith Cavell and a stop at some lakes before returning to the Lodge.

After dinner His Majesty received a package of developed film from an earlier area visited in eastern Canada en route west, but there were many short rolls of film that needed splicing before viewing. After his secretary placed a phone call to the manager, head bellman Russel Lowden, who showed the Lodge's films, arrived at the cabin with his equipment. It was quite a family scene as the group sat around for half an hour chatting, while Lowden and King George occupied a centre table splicing film. His Majesty put Lowden completely at ease, talking together as they worked. Finally the job was completed and the group was treated to a home picture show. At the request of the King, Lowden then showed the royal couple a number of films about the park.

Two years later the Duke of Kent, younger brother of the King, stayed for three days at JPL. The Duke was very active: if he wasn't riding a horse he was swimming in Lac Beauvert; if he wasn't swimming, he was hiking. His stay was a brief stop on a busy tour of Canada, studying the British Commonwealth Air Training Plan. His smiling informality, including taking his meals in the main dining room and stopping his horse frequently for photographers, made him a hit with the guests and staff.

While the Duke was staying in Point Cabin, Charlie Lambe was assigned as his personal waiter to look after the Duke's meals taken at the cabin. The Duke asked Lambe if he had not seen him before. "Yes, Your Royal Highness, I used to serve your meals at Ciro's Club in London, five years ago," replied Lambe.[3] This led to several chats during the Duke's stay. Over his final pot of tea before leaving, the Duke presented Lambe with a pair of silver cuff links bearing the Duke's personal crest.

For many decades Jasper National Park was known among film-makers as the "Hollywood of the North." The first feature movie filmed in the park was *The Country Beyond*, in 1927. Jasper was chosen when Jack Wooltenholme, assistant director to the Fox Company, saw a brochure advertising what was known then as "the Triangle Tour" (Jasper, Prince Rupert, Vancouver). Within a few days his crew and cast were in Jasper. Fred Brewster assembled 98 packhorses to serve the outfit. The lodge figured largely and many scenes were set within its walls. It was even reproduced as a Hollywood set. The Fox architects charted the lodge, inch by inch, photographed it and drew it to scale. The reproduced set, estimated to have cost $35,000 to build, included the animal heads on the walls, the wicker chairs and ticket booths.

Three years later, in 1930, another Fox film was shot in Jasper National Park and in Mt. Robson Provincial Park nearby. The working title was *Red Sky*, but it was released as *Under Suspicion*. Lois Moran was the

Many Jasper men were hired to act as mounted police officers during the filming of Under Suspicion at Maligne Lake in 1930. JASPER-YELLOWHEAD HISTORICAL SOCIETY

star. At one point Miss Moran was busy with interior scenes, and Betty Smith, an employee in the lodge's gift shop, was chosen to double for her during some scenes at Mt. Robson.

The spring of 1946 found the Lodge enjoying its first season since closing for the war. The staff were even preparing to open three weeks earlier than usual for a group of about 200 people from the Paramount movie company. They were preparing to film scenes for *The Emperor Waltz*, starring Bing Crosby and Joan Fontaine. The Canadian Rockies were being substituted for the Alps of the Austrian Tyrol. An advance group of directors, producers and department heads arrived in Jasper on the 24th of May to scout the locations, assisted by park superintendent Wood and other park officials. A few days later a special train brought the rest of the crew and cast to town.

Billy Wilder was one of the directors of *The Emperor Waltz*, which cost $3 million to make. The cast and crew were well-received by the guests and employees of the Lodge, and by the townspeople. Saturday and Sunday afternoons would see a lot of locals driving out to the locations to watch the filming. Bing Crosby was a local favourite, both because of his passion for golf and fishing, and because of his sincere, relaxed manner with everyone.

Crosby became so enamoured of the golfing and fishing that Wilder

Bing Crosby watches Tyrolean dancers practice on the Lodge golf course during the filming of The Emperor Waltz in 1946. JASPER-YELLOWHEAD HISTORICAL SOCIETY

had guards posted at all strategic outlets to make sure that Bing didn't wander off the set when, in Bing's opinion, his "weather sense" was better than that of the barometer or light meter. He returned to play in the Totem Pole golf tournament three times.

On one visit Bing went out sheep hunting with some outfitters. Caught in a high wind and heavily-falling snow, they dismounted to shelter behind some rocks. Feeling sorry for Bing, who was shivering, wet and looked awfully miserable, the outfitter asked, "Anything you want, Mr. Crosby?" "As long as I have a wish," said Bing, "I wish Hope was here."[4]

Bing rarely passed up an informal opportunity to sing, whether in the dining room, the staff recreational hall or at a function in town. Once, when passing a table in the dining room, he overheard a youngster from Oklahoma say to his parents, "Gee, I wish he would sing." Bing promptly swung around, mounted the orchestra stand and sang for 20 minutes.

After the filming of *The Emperor Waltz* was completed, director Wilder needed 30 lodgepole pines to take back to Hollywood to use as backdrops during his studio shooting. The superintendent had to wire to Ottawa for permission, which was denied. It's thought that Wilder dug them up anyway, at night.

Between June and October of 1953, Jasper buzzed with movie stars

Corinne Calvet, a star in The Far Country *in 1953, poses as a bicycle waitress.* JASPER-
YELLOWHEAD HISTORICAL SOCIETY

once again. There were two dramas involving some of the biggest movie stars of the day, one full-length musical, and a 3-D adaptation of a novel by Emile Zola. The titles are memorable: *Rose Marie*, a musical by Metro-Goldwyn-Mayer; *River of No Return*, by 20th Century-Fox featuring Marilyn Monroe and Robert Mitchum; Universal-International's *The Far Country*, starring Ruth Roman, Corinne Calvet, James Stewart and Walter Brennan; and *The Human Beast*, with Rita Hayworth. The movie stars and production crews stayed at the Lodge. For every featured star there were perhaps 15 behind-the-scenes people: prop men, makeup people, dramatic coaches, wardrobe people, publicity and script writers, electricians, sound engineers, cameramen, carpenters, security officers, technicians and directors.

In 1974, when Patty Hearst was wanted by police authorities, someone thought that they had seen her at the Lodge. A woman answering her description was seen in the dining room, and she seemed to be staying in a cabin that had no guests registered. Security guards and police were summoned, the surrounding cabins were evacuated and the area cordoned off. A very frightened young woman was called out. She was not Patty Hearst, but a guest who had decided to stay on for a few days when her family moved out. The register wasn't up-to-date.

In addition to famous clientele, the Lodge has its own ghost — a friendly unseen one. It resides in Point Cabin. It must be afraid of the dark, because the lights sometimes mysteriously come on in the cabin after someone has turned them off and left.

6   The Silver Totem Pole

A person would have a hard time finding another golf course in the world to rival the one at Jasper Park Lodge. Most golfers concede that it's not a particularly tough course, but it's sometimes hard to concentrate on a shot when there's such beautiful scenery all around. Although many other courses have natural hazards, few have live handicaps in the form of bears, elk or coyotes!

The present course had pretty rough beginnings back in 1922. In that year the Dominion Parks Branch decided to build a course in the vicinity of Lac Beauvert for the use of visitors and townspeople. Charlie Duncan, a golf professional from Banff, laid out a simple nine-hole course. Very little progress was made in that first year. There was a lot of thick bush to clear and the ground was a mass of boulders, difficult to move with only horses and wagons. Great progress, though, was expected in the summer of 1923. But the appropriation from the park's budget was so small that the engineers could only employ a few teams and wagons. A small camp was erected, and a few men were hired, including a foreman and cook.

A few weeks later the cook was having problems because the men were complaining about his meals. One day the men came in and found the table laid out with knives, forks and plates, but on each plate there was only a handful of oats and a bit of hay . . . and no cook to be found! He asked for his pay, received it, and left town.[1]

Shortly after building Jasper Park Lodge the CNR approached the government, in 1924, offering to take over the golf course. They brought in Stanley Thompson, a noted golf architect from Toronto. Thompson came from a family of distinguished golfers, two brothers having been amateur champions of Canada. He laid out an elaborate 18-hole course, estimated to cost $80,000 to construct.

The terrain had many natural advantages: there was no clay, and the gravelly subsoil ensured good drainage. Plenty of sand was available nearby, and there was good access to water. The site was cleared that first summer by the work of nearly 200 men and 50 teams of horses. Rocks dug and blasted out to create the fairways were used as the foundations for many of the built-up bunkers, tees and greens. The men worked right on through the winter and into the following spring. The one problem was that the soil was too poor and thin for growing good grass. There was good farmland near Edmonton, however, so the CNR purchased a quarter-section of land and stripped it of topsoil, which they hauled to the railway at Stony Plain (west of Edmonton) and put into freight cars. In Jasper it was reloaded into wagons and dumped on the golf course. Nearly 40 carloads were brought in.

A small concrete dam, capable of holding 190,000 L (50,000 gallons) of water, was built about a kilometre up the mountainside, from which water was piped down to the fairways. It took quite a few trips with packhorses to haul the cement up there. The water was also used for drinking, and advertised as pure "Signal Mountain Water."

One time a group of workmen were repairing the pipeline carrying water from the dam to the lodge. They left a few "permanent" lunch supplies, such as jars of jam and honey, in some pipes on the site, thus hoping to fool the bears. They even pushed the jars way down in the pipes.

Tallying up the score on the golf course. CANADIAN NATIONAL

But the next morning the jam and honey were gone. Looking at the pipes, they figured that the bears must have rolled them about until the jars worked down to the end and came out.

The old tin-lined tee boxes on the course, which held water to wash the ball and sand to tee it up, were unique. They were built of small logs, rather complementing the construction of the cabins and lodge. There were benches and drinking fountains of similar construction at many locations. Near the 10th hole there is still the original "wishing well," where golfers may pause and rest awhile. At each of the tees there was also a stone monument from which the length of the hole was given to the centre of the green.

The 13th green was hidden from the sight of golfers approaching it, so a bell was put up on the site, to be rung when the players were finished. The first bell was the original one from Engine #60, the first locomotive to arrive in Jasper on the Grand Trunk Pacific Railway. It was later stolen, and unfortunately has had to be replaced more than once.

The course covers about 35 ha (85 acres). The large scale of the course is similar to the National Links of the U.S.A. at Southampton, Long Island, while the modern scale of lengths and bunkering treatment is like that at Gleneagles, one of the more notable courses in Great Britain. It is actually laid out on the British principle, with the ninth hole farthest from the clubhouse. An additional three holes, added in 1950, permit a nine-hole game, though, without the necessity of golfers cutting in on other players on their way back to the clubhouse. Many of the holes are lined up with the mountain peaks around. For instance, to play the second hole properly, the golfer should aim at the "nose" of the Old Man of the Colin Range, Roche Bonhomme. The holes have such distinctive names as Signal Dip, Colin's Clout, Elk's Wallow, Bear's Den, The Maze, Bad Baby, Cleopatra, and The Climber. The hole and fairway known as Cleopatra were reconstructed at one point because it was felt that the contours of the land were "too suggestive" in association with the name.

The course was officially opened on July 17, 1925, by Earl Haig, commander in chief of the British Forces in World War I. He was also a former captain at the Royal and Ancient Golf Club in St. Andrews, Scotland. The official party consisted of the Earl and Countess Haig, Brigadier-General J. A. Blair, Brigadier-General A. F. Home, Mr. Walter Pratt, general manager of the CN's hotel department, Mr. Thompson, and Colonel Maynard Rogers, the park superintendent.

Prior to the opening ceremonies the Earl inspected a group of mountain guides, park wardens and dining car crew, all war veterans. Many of the mounted men had ridden 80 to 160 km (50 to 100 miles) for the occasion, and were headed by Major Fred Brewster. Haig was presented with a pair of buffalo hair chaps, and Countess Haig received a pair of Indian-made buckskin gauntlets.

When Haig inaugurated the course, he drove the ball about 90 metres

(100 yards) down the first fairway. The caddies, lined up on the fairway, scrambled to retrieve the first ball, a custom followed at the parent course in St. Andrews, Scotland. A freckle-faced lad of 14 retrieved the ball and received a $5 bill from Haig. The ball was later presented to Haig on a silver mount. Countess Haig then shot a ball to land within a few metres of her husband's. In the opening day match he teamed up with Thompson to defeat Blair and Home. On the first hole a black bear ambled away with one of the golf balls. The rules of the game made no provision for this, but it was decided to call it a "rub of the green."

Sir Henry Thornton spent many hours on the course whenever he was in Jasper. He played quite a good game and was particularly known for his smashing drive. But one time he wasn't very lucky:

> Sir Henry's ball had landed in a clump of trees and his position was hopeless; so hemmed in with timber was he that it looked as if he would have either to pick up or lose heaven knew how many strokes ploughing his way out. Other players had stopped, curious as to what he would do. He hesitated for a moment, looking at the appalling lie of the ball. Then he made up his mind — it was no good being President of the Canadian National Railways for nothing — and spoke a word to the caddy. The boy put down his bag and started off for the club house at the double. Presently he came running back, with two men following him, carrying a crosscut saw. A few minutes later a large tree crashed to the earth and Sir Henry took his mashie. There was one less tree at Jasper, but the President won his hole. [2]

The first Totem Pole Tournament was held in 1926, with only 20 participants. It used to signal the end of the season at the Lodge in the early years, but with the season now extending into October this is no longer true. The tournament always began on the second Saturday in September, with the finals on the following Saturday. From 1929 to 1958 the tournament was ably managed by Bruce Boreham, the CNR's public relations agent in Winnipeg.

In the early days selected cities were allocated a limited number of applicants, and competition was keen just to be accepted. One year the president of a large company phoned up President Gordon of the CNR, saying that if he didn't get in the following year, his next ten trainloads would go via CPR . . . he didn't get in. When the field was small many extra events were added to keep the golfers busy. But, as the field grew, these events were dropped.

All of the events during the week featured prizes. One of the unique events was the Inter-Province and State Match, in which teams of six players from various provinces and states competed against other teams. Mixed foursomes and ladies' events were also held. The prizes included: a silver replica of a tee box, which could hold 100 cigarettes; miniatures of the trophy in gold and silver, which made beautiful watch chains; a silver rose bowl for the ladies' events; gold and silver medals, and even totem-pole candlesticks. There was also a "Hole-in-One" medal for such a shot during the tournament.

In the early years of the Totem Pole Tournament all of the golfers arrived by train. CANADIAN NATIONAL

Of course, the grand trophy was the Silver Totem Pole, which featured a 45-cm (18-inch) replica of a totem pole cast in silver and set in an ebony base. There were also four miniature replicas of bears, one set on each corner of the base. The trophy is held for one year by the club to which the winner belongs, and the winner receives a smaller replica to keep. The original trophy was destroyed in the fire in 1952, but a replica has been made.

The lieutenant-governor in Alberta, J.C. Bowen, opened the tournament for many years and handed out the trophies and prizes at the end. John Craig, a CNR official, often led the tournament parade around the Lodge grounds dressed in his kilt and followed by the highland pipe band and golfers.

Shortly after the tournament was started the Lodge hosted the 1929 championship of the Royal Canadian Golf Association. In preparation for it the course was reconstructed in 1928-29, and a clubhouse was built. Jack Milligan, the head groundskeeper, came to work on the course at that time (he retired in 1985 and passed away in 1993). There was a crew of 120 men and 60 teams of horses. They dug up soil from near Lake Edith and added it to the course. Carloads of rotten manure

Page Boys Jack Reilly and George Dixon hold the prestigious Silver Totem Pole golf trophy. CANADIAN NATIONAL

were brought in from packing plants in Edmonton, which were giving the stuff away. Horace Purdy was the head greenskeeper at the time; he also worked as an architect under Thompson.

After the official championship the local golfers held their own tournament and vied for many titles: Box Car Avenue Champion, Sleeping and Dining Car Champion, Maligne Canyon Champion, Baggageroom Champion, Balsam Avenue Champion and Telegraph Pole Champion.

Bing Crosby won the Totem Pole tournament in 1947. JASPER-YELLOWHEAD HISTORICAL SOCIETY

The hero of the JPL course has to be Bing Crosby. While working on the movie *The Emperor Waltz*, being filmed in the park, Bing was on the greens every opportunity he had. The following year, which was 1947, Bing came back to play in the tournament. Almost everyone has a story about Bing when he was in Jasper, but without a doubt the final play was exciting. Bing was in the final with Gordon Verley, of Victoria, British Columbia, and they were all square on the 36th hole:

> Verley was only about a foot from the pin on his third while Bing's second lay beyond the green, at least 30 feet astray of the mark. From this position Bing couldn't even see the pin. He was under the shade of a massive Douglas fir. To make matters more despairing a youngster maintained constant squirming just behind him. The Hollywood ace took his stance then broke it with a good-humoured offer to change places with the lad. This little act cut the tension for the big gallery and Bing followed up by almost nonchalantly chipping the ball into the cup. '

Bing later apologized to Verley for being so lucky!

During the tournament Bing had made a promise to his caddy during a practice round — a new suit for every birdie on the 18th hole. He had to make good three times.

Bing was back again in 1949 when he placed second to his friend G. Coleman, of Miami, Oklahoma, a wealthy banker and rancher. Verley finally won the trophy in 1957, and finished in second place on four other occasions.

Many notable golfers have swung their clubs on the JPL course: many members of the Royal Canadian Golf Association, such as George S. Lyon, R. C. H. Cassels, Paul J. Myler, Major W. D. Wilson, B. C. Anderson; W. Norman Boase, of the Royal and Ancient Golf Club; C. Ross Somerville, former Canadian and U.S. Amateur Champion; and golf greats such as Ben Hogan, Stan Leonard and Marlene Stewart Strait.

Viscount Montgomery, known to everyone as "Monty," who was commander in chief of the British forces after Haig, also enjoyed a few rounds of golf on his visit. An aide arrived with a motorcade to escort him on a drive to Mt. Edith Cavell, but Monty waved him away, saying, "I can see the mountain from here. Very nice. Now which way is the golf course?"[4]

The caddy jobs were very prestigious and sought-after. There were from 40 to 60 caddies. They received free room and board, but the only wages they received were the fees from the golfers. In 1940 the caddy fees were 50¢ to 75¢. At the time greens fees were $3 per day and $15 per week. Caddy fees increased to $2 for 18 holes in 1957, and greens fees also went up to $4 per round or per day and $24 per week. The caddies were required to wait in the "caddy-shack" near the clubhouse, and only came when called. Competition was fierce, but on the other hand, if the golfer was a notoriously poor tipper, it was amazing how many caddies had to go to the bathroom at the same time!

Jim Hogan, a Jasper boy who later became the Canadian Junior Champion, started as a caddy at JPL. Another caddy was so well liked that a wealthy patron took him under his wing and sent him through university. Caddies were phased out in the 1960s, to be replaced by golf carts rented at the pro shop. The pro shop is part of the new clubhouse built in 1968.

Oftentimes the golf professionals had to put up with (or put down) golfers who weren't as good as they thought they were. One such golf pro, Jimmie Rimmer, ended up betting a man that he could play left-handed and still win . . . he did, to the tune of $10,000.

The Lodge was closed from 1942 through 1945 owing to the war. The golf course was left untended, and because it hadn't been watered or weeded it was necessary to plough it up in 1943. It was reseeded in 1945. During the war Jack Milligan, assistant greenskeeper at that time, was sent to work at CN's Minaki Lodge in Ontario, which hadn't closed down. He continued to work at both lodges until 1958, when he returned to JPL to take over from W. H. "Pop" Brinkworth, who'd been there since 1936. Rae Milligan, Jack's daughter, grew up with a golf club in her hand and was the Alberta amateur champion many times, as well as a member of the Canadian team.

The fickle weather causes the greenskeeper more than a few head-
aches at JPL. Mr. Milligan says that the frequent chinooks of the Athabasca
Valley are the real problem. If there's sufficient snow to cover the ground,
or even if the ground is bare, the grass will survive the winter. But when
there's a chinook and the snow melts, then freezes, there can be a tremendous grass kill, as in 1959 when there was a 98% kill that required total
reseeding of the course. Millions of litres of water each week, over 100 lawn
sprinklers and a couple of dozen assistants keep the course green
throughout the summer season.

The Lodge golf course has live handicaps in the form of bears who steal golf balls!
CANADIAN NATIONAL

The live hazards not found at other courses are both a source of
frustration and of fascination on the JPL course: deer and elk, whose
grazing and sharp hooves tear up the grass; bears that take showers in the
sprinklers; flocks of Canada geese feeding on the greens; and bears,
coyotes and ravens that steal golf balls. A 3½ metre (12-foot) high fence
was built around the bushy areas of the course in an attempt to keep the elk
out, and it is fairly successful. The bruins were fascinated by the watering
system. They sometimes chewed the rubber hoses, but were especially
attracted to the sprinklers. The taps' T-handle frequently leaked, emitting a
hissing sound, maybe reminiscent of a bee, and the bears kept pawing at the
handle, eventually turning the water on. Jack had to assign a man just to
follow the bears around to turn off the sprinklers! Organic fertilizer used on
the greens was also attractive to the bears. They'd root up the greens until
the landscape at some holes looked like lunar craters. At various times,
park wardens have been kept busy removing bears from the area.

Bing and the bruin. CANADIAN NATIONAL: RAY O'NEILL

Most golfers have no problems, though, with the animals, because, as one golfer put it, "if you wait long enough they'll move away of their own accord, which is more than can be said of a bunker."

7 Saddle Sores and Mountain Climbing

In a letter to Fred Brewster in 1924 a woman wrote that "a glance at the beautifully painted map in the rotunda of the Lodge convinced us on the morning of our arrival at this greatest national park that not to follow the trails ahorse would be like visiting Paris and avoiding the Louvre and Versailles, or going to London and missing her Westminster Abbey and museums . . . the lure of your faithful trail-horses is the very life of Jasper."[1] And Fred Brewster was the very life of trailriding at Jasper Park Lodge.

While freighting and packing on the GTPR line, Fred Brewster recognized the potential of outfitting tourists. With this in mind he explored the Yellowhead region. In 1912 he decided to settle in Fitzhugh (now

Major Fred Brewster, ca. 1933.
CANADIAN NATIONAL

Jasper), which he described as "a boulder strewn flat with a second growth of lodgepole pine about four feet high." Fred, along with his brothers Pat, George and Jack, were joined by their sister Pearl and her husband, Phil Moore. Together they formed Brewster & Moore Ltd., in 1912.[2]

In the late summer of 1915 Fred volunteered for war service, and left his brother Jack managing the company's outfitting and freighting interests. They had a corral and stables at the rear of the townsite. During that time Jack bought Tent City from Robert Kenneth. When Fred returned, now a major, they began operating the tent camp. In the same year (1919) Colonel Moore, also returned from the war, left the company, which became known as Brewster Brothers.

The Brewsters used "tally-hos" to transport guests from the railway station to Tent City. A tally-ho was a large horsedrawn omnibus, capable of carrying up to 16 people; the name was derived from its British birthplace, where a trumpeter always sat next to the driver and announced the coach's arrival with appropriate fanfare. In early 1921 the Brewsters added a type of large, open motor bus, probably converted from a tally-ho, and within a few years obtained seven cars. In later years Fred also ran buses for sightseeing tours.

The year 1922 saw many changes. The tent camp lease was sold to the CNR, but Fred retained the outfitting and guiding rights for guests at the Lodge, and Jack started his own business near Mt. Robson.

In 1924 Jack initiated the "Glacier Trail" horseback trip from Jasper to Lake Louise.[3] The journey took three weeks one way. Jack would leave from JPL in early July and return six weeks later, in August. In Lake Louise he usually picked up a new group for the return trip. They travelled via Maligne Lake and Maligne Pass to Camp Parker (near the Banff/Jasper park boundary) and from there followed the route of the present Icefields Parkway to Lake Louise. Stops were made at 12 different camps, which included a three-day layover near Mt. Castleguard for a few days' exploration of the fringe of the Columbia Icefield. By 1927 the trip was very popular, but it was hit hard during the Great Depression and was discontinued.

Day trips from the Lodge were very popular, especially during the 1920s and 1930s, the heyday of the trail horse. Trips from two to four hours cost $2.50 in 1927. These short rides went to Maligne Canyon, along the Miette River, to the confluence of the Maligne and Athabasca Rivers, or to Old Fort Point. Full-day trips in the same year cost from $4 to $6; there were return trips to Signal Mountain, The Whistlers, Caledonia Lake, and to Buffalo Prairie and Wabasso Lake.

The Lodge management recommended that strenuous saddle trips should be undertaken only with a guide, whose services cost $7 per day and $4 per half day. For camping trips personal effects were limited to 9 kg (20 pounds), and blankets could be rented for $1 per week, per pair, and Fred provided "everything but a toothbrush and pyjamas." Fred Brewster had a

In 1925 the first meeting of the Jasper squadron of the Trail Riders of the Canadian Rockies was held near Jasper Park Lodge.
PARKS CANADA

transportation desk in the Lodge where guests could register for any of his trips.

In 1925 Fred organized a Jasper squadron of the Trail Riders of the Canadian Rockies from his concession at Jasper Park Lodge. The first camp was held at Mildred Lake, beside the Lodge. In an outdoor ceremony on the eighteenth of July, Mr. and Mrs. Lewis Swift, pioneer homesteaders in the park, and the Earl and Countess Haig, were the first to sign the roll. The Haigs, of course, were at the Lodge to open the new golf course. Mr. J. Murray Gibbon, secretary of the club, presented badges to the various signees (some 75 in total) for miles ridden. Later in the season Sir Henry Thornton also joined. The first grand pow-wow and organizational meeting was held that night in the recreation hall at JPL. The club initially offered

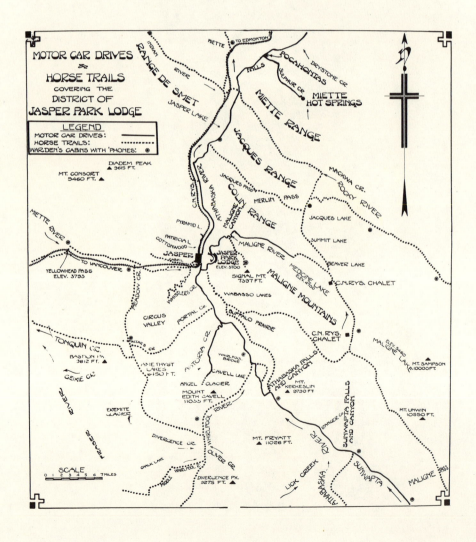

three- and five-day rides, but due to enormous interest they increased the length to eight- and twenty-five days.

Earl Haig refused a complimentary 2,500-mile (about 4000 km) trailrider button, saying that he'd sooner earn a bronze one for 50 miles (80 km). Given a map he marked down the 20 miles that he had ridden while in Banff, and while in Jasper he made a point of riding another 30 miles to qualify for the button.

Beginning in 1928, with the assistance of the railway, Fred leased a parcel of land on the shore of Medicine Lake to be used in conjunction with his Sky Line Trail Rides. The Medicine Lake Chalet became the first in a series of camps and chalets known as "Fred Brewster's Rocky Mountain Camps." They were bases for riding, hiking, boating, mountain climbing, and fishing. Camps at Maligne Lake, in the Little and Big Shovel Passes and in Tekarra Basin were used for his popular Sky Line Rides. He also had a camp in the Tonquin Valley. The Black Cat Ranch near Entrance, east of the park, was also a base for trail rides in the summer and for hunting trips in the fall.

The 105 km (65 mile) return trip to Maligne Lake was very popular. The first night was spent at the Medicine Lake Chalet, and Maligne Lake was reached on the second day. A journey could even be made down the lake by boat. The return trip was via the Sky Line Trail through Shovel Pass. In the first few years the riders dropped down into the Athabasca Valley to Wabasso Lake, and thence back to the Lodge. But around 1930 Fred started cruising the Maligne Ranges looking for a more interesting route back to Jasper than the 16 km (ten miles) through monotonous forest that the Wabasso route entailed. In 1933 he made two trips with horses along the new route, and by 1937 the trail along the crest of the mountains, dropping right down to the Lodge, was sufficiently developed to bring the first paying riders over it. Fred took 19 riders over the trail that year, and by 1941 had taken a total of 153 riders over it. Today the route is among the most popular in the Rockies with both trailriders and hikers.

By 1950 the Maligne Lake Chalet had grown to consist of two log buildings, five cabins and eight frame tents. They were equipped with wood-burning stoves and hot and cold running water. The rates were $8 per day in the tents and $12 per day in the cabins, including food.

Fred also offered many other saddle trips. Two-day trips to Medicine Lake (55 km or 34 miles return) and Athabasca Falls (66 km or 41 miles return) cost $20 per day for one person and $14 per day for two to five persons in 1940. The three-day trip to Jacques Lake cost the same. There were three longer saddle trips: Columbia Icefield to JPL (seven days); JPL to Berg Lake via the Tonquin Valley and then to the railroad at Robson (11 days), and the North Boundary Trail to Mt. Robson, starting at the Black Cat Ranch.

On the longer trips there were few permanent camps, and a new camp was established each night. One wealthy gentleman from the United States

A group of riders ready for the trail, ca. 1925. PROVINCIAL ARCHIVES OF ALBERTA A11288

was rather put off when he heard of this "inconvenience," but he was downright horrified when he found out that there would be no toilet facilities. He delayed going out on the trip until he had ordered and received a "porta-toilet" from home!

Major Brewster, as he was known to all, became a legend in Jasper. Guests knew that they were going to be well-taken-care-of when outfitted by him. He was even known to occasionally serve fresh grapefruit for breakfast on the trail, in a bowl of ice chopped from a glacier near camp! Rocky Mountain Camps was a large operation. Fred employed nearly 50 people and ran a herd of about 300 horses. He even hired someone just to herd his horses in the vicinity of the Lodge all summer.

Beginning in the 1940s a new event was popular during the summer season — the "breakfast ride." This was a half-hour in the saddle near the Lodge, followed by an open-air breakfast on the shore of one of the nearby lakes. There were also "evening steak rides."

Brewster was kept quite busy outfitting for mountain climbing parties as well. Following the example of the Canadian Pacific Railway in Banff and Glacier National Parks, the CNR had brought their own Swiss guides to Jasper Park Lodge in 1924.

In that year Albert Streich and Hans Kohler arrived in Jasper. Streich was the son of noted guide Kaspa Streich, who was killed in the Caucasus in

Europe in 1889. Kohler's father was Niklaus Kohler of Meiringen, Switzerland, the chief guide of the Haslital Valley. The CNR advertised of Kohler and Streich that "they can both speak English fluently and are acquainted with cheesemaking and timber cutting."[4] Streich was also an accomplished skater and skier. They both assisted at the Alpine Club of Canada's camp at Mt. Robson in 1924.

Hans Fuhrer was a Swiss mountain climbing guide, hired by the CNR, who worked out of Jasper Park Lodge.
JASPER-YELLOWHEAD HISTORICAL SOCIETY

The brothers Hans and Heinrich "Heinie" Fuhrer were also imported by the CNR and stationed at Jasper Park Lodge. Their brother, father, grandfather and great-grandfather were all guides in Switzerland. Hans had guided since he was 13 and had come to the United States in 1915. He worked first at Mt. Hood in Oregon, and then for many seasons at Mt. Rainier, where he guided over 100 parties to the summit. In 1923 he became an American citizen and married a Swiss girl there. After coming to Canada to guide, the brothers continued to return to Oregon in the winter, where they operated a dairy farm near Portland.

In 1925 members of the Japanese Alpine Club made their first excursion to the Canadian Rockies, sponsored by their crown prince. Guided by Heinie Fuhrer, Hans Kohler and Jean Weber (a skilled amateur of the Swiss

Alpine Club who also worked at JPL), they made the first ascent of Mt. Alberta. Assisted by five trailmen and 40 horses supplied by Fred Brewster, they carried scientific instruments, still- and motion-picture cameras, and a complete field darkroom for photographic work.

One of the biggest climbing seasons was in 1928, when the Sierra Club stayed at the Lodge and climbed Mt. Edith Cavell; club members also climbed in the Tonquin Valley and the Mt. Robson regions. In the Tonquin, Heinie Fuhrer led ascents of Bastion Peak four days in a row, beginning at three o'clock each morning. The club was very impressed by the Fuhrer brothers, stating that "they exhibited superb ability and extreme courage at all times on the climb [of Robson]."[5] They were also described as "two of the worthiest guides that ever yodelled." In the same year Jean Weber guided parties up Mt. Leah at Maligne Lake, Pyramid Mountain, and Mt. Edith Cavell.

In 1930, Kitty Götsch-Trevelyan climbed Mt. Edith Cavell with Hans Fuhrer, one of the first women to do so. Kitty was the daughter of a prominent British politician and spent a number of months hitchhiking and walking across Canada. She had camped about a kilometre from the Lodge and had applied for a job there. The manager, John O'Brien, was impressed by her travels, but had no job to offer. Soon the place was buzzing about her travels, and she even met Sir Henry. She had the run of the place: the amusements, cinema, pool and so on. In turn, the management took a photo of her tent to say "she came by our Railway, just think of that!"

Everyone was very excited about Kitty's intended climb of Cavell, one of the earliest of the season. Hans was a complete gentleman. When they camped, Kitty rolled her sleeping bag out on the only patch of grass, and Hans did likewise nearby, asking if he was "far enough away." He kept his ice axe beside him in case grizzlies came calling, and even wore a scarlet cap while hiking, to scare them away. On her return, exhausted, Kitty made a deal with the management to let them use her exploit for publicity, in exchange for a bed, bath, huge meals, a nurse to care for her sunburn, breakfast in bed and other amenities. There were seven courses on the evening menu and she ordered them all! Kitty was instantly famous and people at the Lodge, where she lived in luxury over the weekend, came up to shake her hand and congratulate her. The assistant manager won free shaves for three months from the barber, having bet the barber that even with the aid of a telescope he wouldn't see the climbers on the summit.

In 1927 the climbing guides could be hired for $7 per day plus expenses. Local guides were hired for ordinary hiking parties. In the 1940s the following rates applied for hiking trips with a guide: $15 per day for one person, $23 per day for two people, and $7.50 for each additional person. The price included packhorses to help carry food, bedding, tents, camp equipment and personal baggage.

When Yvon Chouinard, Fred Beckey and Dan Doody came to make the first ascent of the north face of Mt. Edith Cavell in the summer of 1961,

Members of the Sierra Club climbed Mt. Robson in 1928. The top figure is guide Hans Fuhrer, followed by Don Woods of Spokane, Washington, guide Heinie Fuhrer, Norman Clyde of Independence, California, and Miss Marion Montgomery of Hubbard Woods, Illinois. CANADIAN NATIONAL

they stayed gratis at JPL, an arrangement that was unheard-of in the post-World-War-Two period. Because they owned only one sports jacket among them, the climbers had to take turns eating in the dining hall.

Although the Canadian National Railways no longer has its own Swiss climbing guides, Jasper is still a mecca for climbers and hikers. And

WHAT TO WEAR

AT THE LODGE—Let your taste be your guide. Wear what you like, but you'll find sports and lounging clothes best for relaxation.

FOR MOTORING—A medium weight coat or wrap is always useful. So are sun glasses. Wear low-heeled shoes unless you just want to sit in the car when you reach a place worth exploring.

FOR RIDING—You can get along without boots or jodhpurs or other special riding togs. Breeches or "levis" are a good idea if you have them. Don't forget a sweater or a warm shirt.

FOR GOLF—What you wear on the course at home. Skirt or slacks, short-sleeved sweater; the proper shoes and gloves.

FOR DAY TIME—That depends on the weather and what you're doing. Suit yourself . . . Just be comfortable.

FOR EVENING—Fuss if you like, it's up to you. Many do—many don't. The only formality at Jasper Park Lodge is that men must wear coat or jacket with tie for dinner and during the evening in the Central Building. Shorts are not worn in the Dining Room. Come prepared for cool mountain evenings.

A page from a promotional brochure ca. the 1950s. CANADIAN NATIONAL

guests can still enjoy hours-long or days-long saddle trips through the mountains.

There have always been many other recreational activities at Jasper Park Lodge besides golf, trailriding and mountain climbing; fishing, swimming, boating and canoeing, bicycling and scenic tours are perenially popular, as well as indoor activities such as dancing and table tennis.

Fishing has always been very popular. The CNR was interested in almost any venture that would increase tourism and thus put more passengers on its railway and more guests into its hotels. With the support of Billy Robinson and Osborne Scott of the CNR, Major Brewster arranged for two biology students from the University of Manitoba to do a survey of Maligne, Medicine, Jacques and Wabasso Lakes in order to determine their ability to maintain fish populations. The report was positive, and in 1928 the first speckled or brook trout fingerlings were released in Maligne Lake, the beginning of an extensive stocking program by the park.

Before long a Maligne River Anglers Club was formed. To obtain membership a fisherman had to catch a brook trout weighing one pound (about 500 grams) or over along the Maligne River between the outlet of Maligne Lake and the inlet of Medicine Lake. The fish could be caught only on an artificial fly, with a single hook, and with a rod of less than six ounces. Qualifying members received a bronze lapel membership button. The angler catching the largest trout of the season received a gold lapel button; the second largest was good for a silver button.

Bing Crosby, as ardent a fisherman as he was a golfer, was elected the Honourary President of the club in 1946. Bing was ecstatic about the honour, saying "I'd sooner accept that gold badge than an Oscar. Anyone can win an Oscar, but very few can win that button."[6] Bob Davis, a New

York *Sun* columnist, outdoor writers Courtney Ryley Cooper and Rex Beach, and humourist Irvin Cobb were others who held the position.

Motion pictures produced by the CNR and the Canadian Government Travel Bureau served to advertise Jasper National Park and the many recreational opportunities to be found there. The first motion picture produced by CN was in 1927. By 1931 their catalogue listed 47 films. Most focussed on the great Canadian outdoors — fishing, hunting, trailriding, winter sports, scenics, and even adventure films shot from the cowcatcher of a locomotive or from the bow of a canoe catapulting through rapids — and many featured JPL and Jasper Park.

One of the most popular outdoor activities was "bear watching." This took many forms, from simply watching them from the five o'clock bus that went to the garbage dump, to actively feeding them to get a better picture or putting a cub in a gunny sack and carrying it around!

Bear watching was a favourite activity at the Lodge for many years.
CANADIAN NATIONAL

The bears frequented the garbage dump, which was used by both the Lodge and the town. The bears sometimes came out to the road to meet the garbage wagon. One of the new garbagemen, discovering that he was being followed by three bears, left his wagon and ran back to town. When he returned with a more experienced fellow, the bears had knocked some of the cans off the wagon, while the horses stood watching them composedly. After the hotel incinerator was built, the bears thought that they'd found heaven and postponed their winter retirement to the hills, instead snuggling up comfortably against the warm walls of the brick incinerator.

Fortunately no one was ever seriously injured in those years, considering some of the silly things that were done. Feeding, harrassing or simply coming too close to a bear (or other wild animals) is a very dangerous thing to do — and has been against park regulations for many years, now.

Besides "bear-watching buses" the transportation services included regularly scheduled sightseeing trips, picnic parties, shopping in town, an evening theatre bus, Sunday morning church bus, privately chauffeured cars for hire, and a taxi service within the Lodge grounds that was heavily used during poor weather. Outings could be arranged at the Local Transportation Desk.

The scenic drive to Mt. Edith Cavell was the most popular of the Lodge's motor drives, ca. 1927. PUBLIC ARCHIVES CANADA PA58544

The following trips (return, with a chauffeur) were offered in 1927: Maligne Canyon ($2.25), Glacier of the Angel Drive to Mt. Edith Cavell ($4.50), Pyramid and Patricia Lakes ($2.75), Henry House Drive ($3.50), and the Pocahontas Drive ($7.00). A long, one-day trip to Maligne Lake

With the opening of the Banff-Jasper Highway in 1940, bus tours to the Columbia Icefield area were offered. CANADIAN NATIONAL

The swimming pool was a popular distraction on those hot summer days.
CANADIAN NATIONAL

and back, including a boat trip, lunch and afternoon tea at the chalet, cost $20 in 1950. In the same year the all-inclusive rental of a Buick convertible, with a uniformed chauffeur, was $50 per day.

The first tennis courts were constructed in the early 1920s, and were considered the equal of championship courts anywhere in the world. Fees in 1927 were 75¢ per hour for singles and $1 per hour for doubles. New courts were built in 1972.

The original swimming pool was built in 1926 of reinforced concrete and measured 30 m (100 feet) by 12 m (40 feet). There was a wading pool at one end and up to 3 m of water at the deep end, suitable for diving. In addition to overhead lighting, electric bulbs beneath the surface illuminated the water. The pool adjoined the boathouse, and spectator benches actually extended over it. A nearby cabin housed the dressing rooms and shower baths. The rooms and showers were rented for 25¢, and bathing suits for 50¢. A new pool was built in 1977.

George O. Stafford, an employee of the hotel department in Montreal, was the man first in charge of the pool. He was a master diver who had come from England, where he was the junior champion of the southern counties. During 1922, 1923 and 1924 he was the Quebec Fancy Diving Champion and was runner-up for the Canadian championship in 1922. In 1924 he won the Canadian Indoor Fancy Diving Championship. His prowess no-doubt enlivened warm afternoons at the JPL pool — a pool with its own pro.

Boating on Lac Beauvert has always been a favourite pasttime. Initially the Lodge owned the rowboats and canoes and rented them directly

Canoes and rowboats could be rented at the boathouse for a leisurely paddle around Lac Beauvert. PROVINCIAL ARCHIVES OF ALBERTA A11286

to guests for 50¢ an hour, but eventually the service was taken over by a concessionaire.

On a calm, sunny day a canoe seems to be suspended in midair, the water in Lac Beauvert is so clear. The clarity of the water is emphasized by the hard-luck story of how the valley lost its private airline:

Some years ago Bill Holland, a veteran bush pilot, figured that there should be a tidy profit flying the Lodge's guests to and from Jasper's far-flung points of interest. He bought a seaplane and cut a swath in the pines at one end of Lac Beauvert. Business was fine, but he had to give it up [because] landing was too dangerous . . . on a calm day Holland couldn't see the water.[7]

Back in the late 1920s there was a rather unusual recreational event held at JPL. A group of wealthy midwestern American farmers arrived for a convention. In the evening they gathered on the lawn for a hog-calling contest, which is quite an art. The manager, Mr. O'Brien, became quite nervous, saying "We can't have this," and "What will the other guests think?" (I wonder what the bear and elk thought.) In spite of his fears, both the hogcallers and the other guests enjoyed the contest.

Be it TV-watching or mountain climbing, or any activity in-between, there's no excuse for being bored while staying at Jasper Park Lodge.

8 Room Service on Two Wheels

No matter where you travel in Canada you'll probably encounter someone who has worked at Jasper Park Lodge. Currently, a staff of almost 600 people — from the reservations clerks and bellmen to gardeners, waitresses, chambermaids and room-service waiters on bicycles — cater to over 35,000 visitors a season. The majority of the staff have been students from colleges and universities across the country.

In 1923 almost the entire university of Alberta men's basketball team worked at JPL. They even had their team uniforms sent out and played an exhibition game against the Jasper girls. Sir Henry Thornton arranged the jobs for these young men. For many decades the only way to get a job at JPL was to be "sponsored" by someone of influence, such as a member of parliament or high-ranking railway official. The story used to be that "you don't sass your waitress out at Jasper . . . she may turn out to be the daughter of the governor-general." And this was partly true, because in 1952 Lady Rose Alexander, daughter of Earl Alexander, former governor-general of Canada, worked at the Lodge, but in the front office, not as a waitress.

Even though some of the staff came from well-to-do families, there was still a definite line between staff and guests. Bob Pitts, a CNR employee for 41 years, vividly recalled his arrival in Jasper in 1928 to work as a room clerk at the Lodge. At that time railway agent Tom McDonough (sporting a white Stetson) met every train that arrived. Pitts was dressed in obviously British attire (he had just emigrated) and carrying new baggage. McDonough mistook him for a guest and escorted him out to one of the Lodge's Buick convertibles. Pitts was very impressed with such service. After depositing Pitts' luggage in the back, McDonough asked, "Do you have a reservation?" "No," said Pitts. "You know," said McDonough, "there's a big convention and they may not have room for you." Pitts replied that although he didn't have a reservation, they were expecting him. This perplexed McDonough until Pitts explained that he had come to accept a job. After a minute's stony silence McDonough roughly removed Pitts' luggage, saying, "do you think we run these sort of cars for people like you? Take the bus!"[1]

Besides summer students, the Lodge employed about 100 permanent staff in the early years, including an orchestra. During the winter the permanent members worked at other CN hotels, such as the Fort Garry Hotel in Winnipeg and the Chateau Laurier in Ottawa. Currently about 60-70 staff are permanently employed, but they work at the Lodge year-round, mostly in the engineering, management, front office, personnel and accounting departments. At first glance there doesn't seem to be much life around the Lodge during the winter months, but a closer look reveals receptionists confirming bookings, accountants scrutinizing bills and budgets, personnel officers screening job applications, and managers working on various plans.

Many of the staff are employed in housekeeping. A local Jasper girl who had helped the manager's wife put the furnishings in the new luxurious Point Cabin in 1928 was assigned as the first chambermaid there. A short while later a guest insisted that she be fired for some small neglect. John O'Brien, the manager, publicly complied, then Mrs. O'Brien transferred her temporarily to Outlook Cabin, certain that even if the guest saw her he probably wouldn't know one maid from another maid.

By 1930 the tourist business was booming. In that year the Lodge had 406 staff and a payroll of nearly $130,000. Then the Great Depression hit. There were large cutbacks, such that by 1933 there were only 222 employees and the payroll totalled only $60,000. The manager received a salary of $3705 annually plus room and board for himself and his family[2] — a good income in those days. Even so, some of the staff made nearly as much as that from tips.

There is a lot of competition for jobs at JPL. As many as 8000 applications are received each year. Some positions are more sought-after than others — bellmen, waiters and waitresses for the prestige and tips, gardening and the golf course for the outdoors. Other than in the accounting and front office positions, most don't require any prior education or experience. Experienced waiters and waitresses are preferred, but since some training is provided and it is a resort atmosphere, more emphasis is placed on a friendly personality.

One of the jobs unique to the Lodge is that of room-service waiter . . . on a bicycle. Cold drinks, glasses and ice, and even single hot meals, are carried high on a tray — a performance worthy of a circus act! At one time other bicycles (actually tricycles) were fitted with warming cabinets for larger hot meals. Now small pickup trucks are used. Bicycles are also used by porters to transport luggage, and by bellmen to guide cars to the cabins.

A visitor to the Lodge recalled working as a room-service waiter one summer, many years ago. After a few months he got to feeling pretty confident about his riding skill, which prompted him to bet a friend that he could carry two trays at once, and ride with no hands. Guests and em-

Room-service waiters deliver orders to the cabins on bicycles — a unique service at the Lodge. CANADIAN NATIONAL

ployees lined up along one of the driveways to watch. He crashed . . . and he was fired!

When the Lodge was only open three to four months each year, university students made up most of the staff and recruitment was relatively easy. But now, with the Lodge open from April through October, recruitment is not so simple because most students must return to school in September. This meant that a second recruitment took place in late July or early August, and it was difficult to get people to come to Jasper for only two months. To alleviate this problem the Lodge has been hiring people who can stay the entire season. These people are looking for permanent jobs, not just summer work, and often consider their positions at JPL to be career starts.

Traditionally most of the staff have come from eastern Canada — from Ontario, Quebec and the Maritimes. But with increased unemployment in western Canada it has been easier to recruit in Alberta and British Columbia. And where at one time only about 25% of staff returned each year, in times of high unemployment there's a return rate of almost 60%.

Each year a small number of highly qualified chefs are brought from outside the country, mainly from Switzerland, England and other European countries. It is difficult to hire good Canadian chefs for only six months, but the chefs from Switzerland can work here during the summer, then return to major ski resorts at home during the winter. Occasionally there are small difficulties, though. Once one of the Swiss chefs had just arrived in Canada. He spoke very little English. An error was made on his first paycheque and he was paid double his normal salary. He must've thought that he had landed in heaven; he immediately went out and bought a colour television set!

Complete accommodation, recreation and social facilities are on hand for JPL staff. There are a number of cabins, mostly shared rooms for singles, although there are some private rooms for couples and singles. There's a cafeteria, snack bar, party room, disco and recreation room. The staff social director organizes activities, newsletters, a yearbook and so on. And there is liberal access to all guest facilities, such as the pool, tennis courts, golf course and trail rides.

Jasper Park Lodge is known as a fun place to work. Many romances have blossomed and marriages have come about. One chauffeur at JPL, a young medical student, met and married the only daughter of a millionaire. Some staff are even second- and third-generation employees.

In earlier years Baxter's soda fountain in town was the "in" place for Lodge staff to hang out. They frequently ordered Mrs. Baxter's chocolate cakes for special occasions. And near the end of the season the staff used to produce a variety show for the guests. There were plays, poems and music. Some of the original music was even later heard on network radio.

Of course, any staff quarters are known to be a bit on the wild side at times, but one of the bus drivers was a little surprised one morning, as he drove by, to see a woman climbing out of a window with just a towel on. He was even more surprised when she kept on running, even when her towel caught on the sill. It turned out that someone had left a door open, and as she stepped out of the shower, she had encountered a black bear in the hallway!

9　Business As Usual

Jasper Park Lodge is a self-contained unit in many ways, a town within itself. The staff live right on the site. There's really everything a guest needs at JPL, from souvenirs and haircuts to movies and church services. There's an efficient transportation system of 58 vehicles, including cars, limousines, service trucks and so on, and 16 bicycles for the bellmen and room-service waiters. The Lodge even has its own mechanics and service station.

Although much of the activity and work of the staff goes on behind the scenes, there are two areas where the work is very visible — in the gardening department and in food services, from the kitchen to the dining table.

The very first gardener at JPL was William Glass. Although Glass had worked as a gardener in England, none of the gardeners have had degrees in horticulture — they simply loved the earth and learned by doing. The vagaries of the mountain climate are many, and through trial and error the JPL gardeners have developed their craft. Little snow cover in winter, bright sun and cool nights even in summer, poor soil and potential frost any day of the year are all factors that stand in the way of a good garden.

Glass learned that the deer waded through the marigolds and nipped the petunias and bulbs. In response, he either didn't plant these species, or he put them in out-of-the-way places. It seemed that the deer didn't like snapdragons and nemesia, though, so those he used in great numbers; they're still common at the Lodge.

When a rock garden was built in front of the lodge in the 1920s, the original intention was to plant a representative collection of alpine plants there. But that didn't work, because the flowering season was too short, and tufts of green vegetation were not of much interest to guests. Besides, Glass felt that the natural arrangement on the alpine tundra was far superior to anything a gardener could produce. The rock garden was never rebuilt after the 1952 fire.

When King George VI and Queen Elizabeth stayed at Jasper Park Lodge in 1939, the Queen was very impressed by the beautiful flower display and inquired of the park superintendent how they could be growing so well in the mountains at the beginning of June. Mr. Glass had grown them in pots in the greenhouse and then stayed up through the night to plant them in the beds just before the royal couple arrived. The Queen, very pleased with the gesture, invited Mr. Glass to the cabin for a chat with her and the King. When the gardener arrived, the Queen herself opened the door. Glass said afterwards that the Queen "knew just as much about plants and flowers as I did." More than 6000 plants were grown for the royal visit.[1]

Three gardeners; three "Bills." Bill Nicholl (who retired in 1990) followed in his father's footsteps. His father, also Bill, had started at JPL as gardens foreman under Glass in 1925, then became head gardener in turn and retired in 1960. Bill worked part-time and after school helping his

During the early 1960s flowers were shipped from the Lodge's greenhouse to other CN hotels in Edmonton, Saskatoon and Port Arthur, Ontario. CANADIAN NATIONAL

father with such chores as raking the lawn. Then in 1947 he was hired on a full-time basis in the greenhouse. After working for the railway in Jasper townsite from 1951 to 1960, he returned to the Lodge to take over from his father.

Bill and one assistant are kept busy throughout the winter, but they're joined by as many as 15 others for the busy summer season. During the winter the greenhouse is a lush, tropical garden compared to the snow and cold outside. The three main jobs in the winter are overhauling equipment and ordering supplies, maintaining and propagating the tropical house plants for the cabins and lodge, and growing bedding plants for the gardens.

A few crew are hired in March and by mid-April Bill has a full complement of staff. The first job is to clean up the grounds of winter debris. If there is major landscaping to do, say around a new cabin, they may thaw the ground early to do the work. Starting in the third week in May they spend almost three weeks planting. Ironically, if the weather is clear and sunny the work takes longer, as half of the crew is kept watering. In cloudy or rainy weather that isn't a problem. If it seems likely that there will be late frosts, planting is first done close to the cabins, not out in the open. There is no underground sprinkler system because of all the television, telephone and gas lines, so everything is watered manually with hoses and buckets.

In the spring Bill and his crew plant approximately 75,000 annuals and 4000 potted plants of about 50 different varieties. They are chosen in harmony with the short growing season (two-and-a-half months if lucky) and the temperature extremes encountered. The commonest varieties are alyssum, begonia, calendula, centaurea, chrysanthemum, coleus, cosmos, dahlia, dusty miller, fuchsia, godetia, geranium, helichrysum, impatiens, lobelia, nasturtium, nemesia, nicotiana, marigold, pansy, petunia and snapdragon.

In June Bill starts planting biennials in the greenhouses for next year. And, as a result of his winter's work, one crop of cuttings comes in each month for bouquets and table settings. In 1984 he provided 1500 centrepieces for tables and many more single flowers. There are often birthday or anniversary requests, with chrysanthemums and carnations the favourites. The bellmen deliver the cut flowers.

Lots of growers come by to talk, and they sometimes ask for cuttings, but Bill has some trade secrets that he doesn't let out.

Probably the busiest locations at Jasper Park Lodge, however, are the kitchens and dining rooms. There are six kitchens (Main Kitchen, Moose's Nook, Henry House, Copper Kettle, Tonquin Room, Staff Kitchen), plus the Belvedere Deck during July and August. In 1984 over 400,000 meals were served to guests and staff. In the middle of the summer nearly 4000 meals are served daily, not counting snacks.

Even in 1969, with only one main dining room, the quantities of food served each day, even by rough estimates, was staggering: 55 L (12 gallons) of cream, 90 L (20 gallons) of ice cream, 100 L (24 gallons) of milk, 45 kg (100 pounds) of butter, 600 to 900 eggs, 65 loaves of bread, 30 loaves of French bread, 75 to 100 pies, 24 layer cakes and 13 kg (30 pounds) of

Hildebrandt, the maître d', makes a waitress inspection, c. 1950. CANADIAN NATIONAL

cookies. Six cases of fresh oranges and three cases of fresh grapefruit were squeezed daily. In addition, the Lodge provided about 600 rolls and muffins for each meal and 1600 cups of coffee and 1600 pots of tea an hour.[2]

The Lodge bakery used to be in a separate building. The story is told of the baker's assistant who had to chase bears out of the bakeshop before he could enter to work in the morning.

Many specialties are brought in from nearby and around the world:

Jasper Park Lodge
JASPER — ALBERTA

Golf Course — 14th Tee

Luncheon

Fruit Cocktail	*Tartine of Salami*
Green Relish	*Iced Apple Juice*

Ox Tail Soup with Barley   *Chicken Broth Garni*
Jellied Madrilene

Shirred Eggs Opera
Steamed Alaska Cod, Melted Butter
Broiled Fresh Lake Trout, M.D.H
Poached Turkey Wing with Rice, Supreme Sauce
Braised Shoulder of Pork, Californienne
Roast Rump of Beef au Jus
Cold B.C. Salmon, Combination Salad
Chopped Chicken Sandwich, Garni
Fruit Plate Chantilly with Raisin Bread

Green Cabbages   *Mashed Turnips*
Mashed,   Boiled   or   Baked   Potatoes

Pear Pie	*Diplomat Pudding*
Stewed Crabapples	*Ice Cream and Cake*

Canadian Cheese

Milk   -   Tea   -   Coffee

Wednesday, July 26., 1950

CANADIAN NATIONAL SYSTEM

no-preservative jams from Switzerland, sockeye salmon from Vancouver Island, Arctic char from the north, buffalo meat from Manitoba, exotic fruits from New Zealand, fresh herbs from an Alberta specialist, and sausages from a small deli in Canmore, Alberta.

With a large turnover of staff, many of them inexperienced, there is a staggering breakage of china and crockery — about 3000 glasses, 500 cups and saucers, and 500 plates per summer.[3] Many broken items result when room-service trays and contents are put out on the lawn by guests for pickup, and they are knocked over by the wind, animals or people.

Although there are many staff working in the kitchens, it wasn't always so. During the 1920s an excursion train arrived from Prince Rupert one day, and the travellers ate at the Lodge. After the meal, of course, there was a large pile of dirty dishes to be washed in one small sink. Luckily, the wife of the lieutenant-governor, who was staying at the Lodge, helped the pantry boy clean up while her husband went to Maligne Lake.

Also, with inexperienced staff, strange things may happen besides the proverbial bowl of spilt soup. During July and August the menu in the Moose's Nook dining room sometimes includes flambés. One year, shortly

The main dining room, ca. 1925. JASPER PARK LODGE

after "flambé season" had started, one of the waiters arrived in the staff linen and uniform room requesting another uniform jacket immediately so that he could go back to work — the back of his original one had been completely scorched!

And, what do you do when a guest requests some food for her children's pet fish? Why, you simply spend half a day phoning around Jasper, searching for someone who has tropical fish, and buy some food from them! That's one specialty the chefs don't keep in stock.

10   Into the Nineties
and Beyond

The year 1988 saw a major corporate change for JPL, when Canadian Pacific Hotels & Resorts purchased Jasper Park Lodge from Canadian National. The new management came with a commitment to turn the Lodge into a year-round resort destination.

With that goal in mind, they began a five-year restoration and development project which was completed in 1994. This involved renovations to all 442 guest rooms and public areas, and the upgrading of 13 meeting rooms with complete convention facilities. Twenty-one of the guest rooms were converted from three former management staff housing units, when new staff housing was constructed. A shopping promenade was constructed on the lower level of the main lodge, with unique boutiques, a nightclub, a lounge, a cafe and a formal dining room. The golf course has also undergone renovations and restorations with the construction of new bunkers and cart paths, and restoration of tee boxes.

The restoration project included the "greening" of the Lodge's energy systems to greatly reduce electrical consumption. Energy efficient lighting has been installed in many areas; electric heaters have been changed to hot water heaters; insulation in walls and ceilings has been improved; and a multitude of other smaller changes have also taken place.

The renovations (particularly the winterization of the over 112 buildings on the property), and the growth of participation in winter sports, has enabled JPL to become a winter destination. As such, the Lodge joins Canadian Pacific's other Rocky Mountain hotels — the Banff Springs Hotel and Chateau Lake Louise — in offering a classic mountain holiday. Depending on the snow conditions, visitors may be able to cross-country ski from their cabin door. Lodge staff maintain a skating area on Lac Beauvert, which attracts visitors and locals alike all winter long.

Jasper Park Lodge has gained a world-wide reputation as a place to have a high-class holiday or convention in close proximity to the natural environment. It is this environmental situation that has attracted visitors from day one, and will continue to do so. The management of the Lodge and Canadian Pacific Hotels & Resorts is well aware of this and strives to maintain the unique atmosphere while incorporating renovations and expansions according to changing lifestyles.

In the coming years the Lodge will continue to develop into a complete resort destination. But whether catering to conventioneers or honeymooners, prime ministers or people-next-door, in summer or in winter, Jasper Park Lodge is dedicating itself to upholding the tradition of providing a high-quality holiday close to nature — a memorable place and experience.

Notes

Chapter 1: Grand Schemes for Grand Hotels

1. Public Archives of Canada (hereafter PAC), Parks Canada 1883-1980, RG 84, vol. 523, file J17-GTP-8, Chas. M. Hays to Frank Oliver, 30 March 1911.
2. Hays was also promoting the development of a resort townsite called "Swiftholm," near present Jasper townsite. The lots were offered for sale by the Edmonton firm of Inglis, MacDonald and Thom. Hays, though, went down on the Titanic in April of 1912 and the plan fell through.
3. Canada, "Report of the Superintendent of Jasper Park" in *Annual Report of the Department of the Interior, 1911*, p. 38.
4. PAC, RG 84, vol. 523, file J17-GTP-8, R. H. Campbell to Frank Oliver, 4 April 1911.
5. PAC, RG 84, vol. 522, file J17-GTP-4, G. U. Ryley, 6 March 1909.
6. Wheeler, Arthur O., "The Alpine Club of Canada's Expedition to Jasper Park, Yellowhead Pass and Mount Robson Region, 1911" in *Canadian Alpine Journal (v. 4), 1912*, p. 7.
7. Canada, "Report of the Superintendent of Jasper Park" in *Annual Report of the Department of the Interior, 1915*, p. 57.
8. PAC, RG 84, vol. 522, file J17-GTP-2, letter to H. R. Charlton, 26 February 1915.
9. In 1916 the Grand Trunk Pacific Railway's tracks on the east side of the Athabasca River, east of Pocahontas, were torn up for delivery to France to build lines to carry troop trains. This effectively ended the Château Miette project.

Chapter 2: Tent City

1. The Edmonton Tent and Mattress Company was founded in 1895 by Robert Kenneth. Kenneth brought his equipment by ox train from Calgary, where he had been a tent maker. The firm made tents for settlers, and then business boomed with the Klondike gold rush. The establishment is the oldest of its kind in Edmonton, and still operating as the Edmonton Tent and Awning Company.
2. Fred Brewster, part of the family that was already so well-known in Banff National Park, came to the Yellowhead region in 1910. He freighted and packed for the construction crews of the railway. In 1911 he recognized the tourist potential of the area, and with his brother Jack and brother-in-law Phil Moore, established an outfitting business in Jasper.
3. PAC, RG 84, vol. 466, township land register, p. 508. The Edmonton Tent and Mattress Company didn't apply for their lease until 1 April 1917, and were then granted a five-year lease for the 0.83-hectare (2.05-acre) site.
4. PAC, RG 84, vol. 522, J17-GTP-2, H. R. Charlton to J. B. Harkin, 19 March 1915.
5. Canada, "Report of the Superintendent of Jasper Park" in *Annual Report of the Department of the Interior, 1919*, p. 23.
6. Hopper, A. B. and Kearney, T., *Synoptical History of Organization, Capital Stock, Funded Debt and Other General Information*, CNR, Montreal, 1962.
    On 6 June 1919, the Canadian National Railways Company was incorporated to provide a company by which the activities of the companies under the Canadian Northern Railway system and the Canadian Government Railway might be operated as a national system. All deeds, leases, agreements and documents requiring execution under seal continued to be drawn under the respective corporate names (pp. 219-220). The operation and management of the Grand Trunk Pacific Railway system was entrusted to the Canadian Northern Railway Company on 12 July 1920, so that the GTPR system could be operated in harmony with the Canadian National Railways System. The year 1923 saw the practical amalgamation of the railways, but it wasn't until 11 May 1956, that 18 companies, including the Canadian Northern Railway Company and the

GTPR, were actually amalgamated under the name "Canadian National Railways Company" and became a legal entity (p. 349).

Chapter 3: A Wilderness Retreat is Built

1. Hopper, A. B. and Kearney, T., *Synoptical History . . .*, 1962.
   Jasper Park Lodge was actually built by the Canadian Northern Railway Company, which was under the umbrella group of the Canadian National Railways (see Chapter 2, note 6).
   A new company, the Canadian National Hotels, Limited, was incorporated on 15 October 1954, whose sole purpose was to acquire and operate all of the hotels in the system. The stock of the following companies was acquired: The Canadian Northern Railway Company (JPL); Canadian National Realties, Limited; The Grand Trunk Pacific Development Company, Limited; Canadian National Railway Company; and Canadian National Hotels, Limited (p. 66).
   "Under agreement dated January 14, 1955 ownership of Jasper Park Lodge, including the golf course and other properties, was transferred to Canadian National Hotels, Limited as of December 31, 1954, in consideration of (a) the issue to Canadian National Railways Company of Capital Stock and Debentures of Canadian National Hotels, Limited having a face value of $5,540,847, representing the amount of investment in Jasper Park Lodge as at January 1, 1954, and (b) cancellation by Canadian National Railway Company of the debt owing to it by The Canadian Northern Railway Company, with respect to advances to the extent of $5,540,846.95." (p. 72)
2. Marsh, D'Arcy, *The Tragedy of Henry Thornton*, MacMillan Co., Toronto, 1935, p. 48-49.
3. Hanbury-Williams, C., "Jasper National Park and the Triangle Tour" in *The Canadian Magazine*, April 1924, p. 392.
4. Jasper-Yellowhead Historical Society (hereafter JYHS), Jasper Park Lodge file.
   After Mr. Slark's death Mrs. Slark continued with his plans by constructing and operating a tea-house and curio shop at Mt. Edith Cavell, which was open until 1972.
5. *Edmonton Journal*, 19 June 1931.
6. "Railways to Keep Resorts Closed" in *Edmonton Journal*, 23 March 1943.

Chapter 4: A Night of Ruin

1. *Lethbridge Herald*, 17 July 1952.
2. Souliere, E. A., "How They Did It At Jasper" in *Canadian National Railways Magazine*, September 1952, p. 7.
3. *Ibid*.
4. Phillips, Alan, in *Maclean's*, 1 September 1953.

Chapter 5: Royalty and Movie Stars

1. *Golf at Jasper Park in the Canadian Rockies*, CNR, Montreal, p. 31.
2. Boreham, Bruce, *Their Majesties Visit Jasper*, June 1939.
3. *Canadian National Railways Magazine*, September 1941.
4. Sutton, Horace, *Footloose in Canada*, Rinehart & Co., New York, 1950, p. 236.

Chapter 6: The Silver Totem Pole

1. JYHS, J. B. Snape file, unpublished manuscript.
2. Marsh, D'Arcy, *The Tragedy of Henry Thornton*, p. 107.
3. *Jasper Tourist News*, 1965.
4. Ayre, Robert, *The Story of Jasper*, n.d., p. 9.

Chapter 7: Saddle Sores and Mountain Climbing

1. "America's Greatest National Park" in *Canadian National Railways Magazine*, October 1925, p. 15.

2. Archives of the Canadian Rockies, M53, f. 21. Fred Brewster papers, "Articles of Association, Brewster & Moore Ltd." 11 June 1912.
3. Both the Canadian National Railways and the Canadian Pacific Railway publicised the Glacier Trail trip, one of the few occasions when they cooperated in a venture.
4. "Guides for Jasper Park Lodge" in *Canadian National Railways Magazine*, June 1915, p. 20.
5. "Up Where the Clouds Begin" in *Canadian National Railways Magazine*, November 1928.
6. "The Crooner Can Fish Too" in *Canadian National Railways Magazine*, July 1946.
7. Phillips, Alan, in *Maclean's*, 1 September 1953.

Chapter 8: Room Service on Two Wheels

1. Provincial Archives of Alberta, phonotape 71.262, interview of Bob Pitts by Naomi Radford.
2. Hobbs, W. H., *Report re Hotel Department*, CNR, Montreal, 14 February 1934.

Chapter 9: Business As Usual

1. Boreham, Bruce, *Their Majesties Visit Jasper*, June 1939.
2. Archives of the Canadian Rockies, M373, f. 1, "Jasper Information Sheet, August 1969."
3. *Ibid*.

Index

About The Author

Cyndi Smith was born and raised on a cattle ranch on the shores of the Red Deer River, in the heart of the Alberta badlands. She spent her childhood roaming the coulees and cutbanks, searching for fossils and wildlife.

Captivated by the outdoors, Cyndi studied biological sciences at the Northern Alberta Institute of Technology, in Edmonton, and through the University of Waterloo in Ontario.

But the Canadian Rockies have been a magnet to Cyndi for over two decades. She moved to Jasper National Park in 1974 and has hardly left the Rockies since.

Since 1980 she has worked for Parks Canada, first as a park naturalist, then as a patrolwoman, and now as a park warden. Cyndi has worked in Rocky Mountain House National Historic Park, and Jasper, Kluane and Banff national parks. Some of her most memorable experiences involved patrolling the backcountry areas on horseback and on foot.

Cyndi started writing in 1979 and her work has been published in various magazines and newspapers. While working as an historic specialist she wrote a pamphlet about the history of Jasper National Park — *People, Places and Events*.

Cyndi's interest in history led her to write *Off the Beaten Track: women adventurers and mountaineers in western Canada*, about fourteen women explorers, writers, artists, mountaineers and trail guides. Cyndi succeeds these women in her vocations.

As a park naturalist Cyndi had introduced many children to the outdoors, an interest which led her to write three coloring and activity books for children: the *Rocky Mountains Coloring Book*, *Dinosaurs of the Alberta Badlands* and the *Rocky Mountains Alphabet Book*. The first two have since been translated into French.

An avid skier, backpacker, sea kayaker, mountaineer and traveller, Cyndi takes every opportunity to explore off the beaten track in Canada's wilderness areas.

Also From Coyote Books

Coyote Books has been a natural and human history publisher in western Canada since 1985. Besides publishing new works we are also bringing classic mountain literature back into print.

The following books are available through your local bookstore, or directly from the publisher.

Off the Beaten Track: women adventurers and mountaineers
by Cyndi Smith, ISBN 0-9692457-2-6
Biographies of fourteen women explorers, writers, artists, mountaineers and trail guides.

The Mountaineers: Famous Climbers in Canada
by Phil Dowling, ISBN 0-9698939-1-4
Chronicles the incredible stories of ten climbers who have faced the challenges of the mountains and met it in their own extraordinary way.

Timberline Tales: Folklore in Verse of the Canadian Rockies
by Jim Deegan, ISBN 0-9692457-8-5
A verse collection filled with robust, humorous, and poignant accounts of Jim Deegan's life and the mythology of the Canadian Rockies.

The Unknown Mountain
by Don Munday, ISBN 0-9692457-4-2
A reprint of the original 1948 story of mountaineering adventure and exploration in the Coast Mountains of British Columbia.

Ballads of the Badlands
by Arthur Peake, ISBN 0-9692457-3-4
Blizzards, cattle roundups, sodbusters, school days, the government, remittance men, Indians, dinosaurs and his beloved Red Deer River Valley were all subjects for Arthur's pen in Alberta in the early 1900s.

Children's Titles

Coyote Books is becoming the leading publisher of inexpensive coloring and activity books on Alberta and Western Canada. We specialize in accurately interpreting the natural and human history of the region for children.

Rocky Mountains Coloring Book
by Cyndi Smith, ISBN 0-9692457-1-8

An educational coloring book about the natural and human history of the Canadian Rockies. Features: common birds, animals and plants; clear captions that assist with species identification; join-the-dots and mazes; creative coloring opportunities. Also available in French (ISBN 0-9692457-6-9).

Rocky Mountains Alphabet Book
by Cyndi Smith, ISBN 0-9692457-5-0

This latest in our series of interactive and interpretive children's books uses phrases and images such as: "A cougar kitten plays with red Kinnikinnick berries" and " A Wolf watches the Wolverine".

Dinosaurs of the Alberta Badlands
by Cyndi Smith, ISBN 0-9692457-0-X

The first educational activity book to interpret the dinosaur hotbed of Canada. Features: the more common dinosaurs found in Alberta; join-the-dots, mazes, matching and other activites; a pronunciation page; scientifically accurate drawings; creative coloring and writing opportunities. Also available in French (ISBN 0-9692457-7-7).